CONT

C000003090

Map references are denoted in the text by ❶ Centrum van Amsterdam
❷ Historisch Amsterdam ❸ Museum Quarter ❹ Amsterdam Locator
❺ Transit Map

amsterdam places to see

For mad and surreal juxtapositions, few capitals approach Amsterdam. It's a place where high culture meets downtown vibe, where Van Goghs vie with museums of cannabis and erotica, where 17th-century palaces rest weightlessly on sand, and cosy smoke-filled *eetcafés* and brown bars compete with cool designer clubs and pubs, funky shops and chic cuisine. With more canals than Venice, Amsterdam counterbalances a picture-perfect 17th-century hauteur with an easy-going village atmosphere and an arts and entertainment scene that's as high-energy as it is cosmopolitan and cutting-edge.

see it places to see

Sights

The Amsterdam Museum ❷ 5A

The recently modernized and re-named Amsterdam Museum (previously Amsterdams Historisch Museum) is a treasure trove of city history. A new and engaging interactive exhibition, Amsterdam DNA, introduces the visitor in 60 minutes to all that has shaped the city into the multi-cultural melting pot of creativity and free thinking that it is today. The museum is housed in the city's former orphanage and families can enjoy the new *Het Kleine Weeshuis* (The Little Orphanage) experience as they step back in time and enter a bustling 17th-century orphanage while trying to avoid being spotted

Artis Zoo has a lot of attractions

I Amsterdam City Card

This great-value culture and leisure pass saves euros all round, with free admission to more than 30 museums and tourist attractions, public transport, a canal tour and 25 per cent discounts at some restaurants. Three-day passes cost €62 (€52/2 days; €42/1 day). Available at tourist information offices, see *www.iamsterdam.nl*

by its residents. Adm. Open 10am-5pm Mon-Fri, 11am-5pm Sat-Sun and hols. Kalverstraat 92, T: 020 523 1822, www.amsterdammuseum.nl

Anne Frank Huis ❶ 2B

The cramped, bare hideaway where Anne Frank, her parents and sister and four family friends lived for 26 months before deportation, and ultimately death in Belsen, is one of Amsterdam's most moving wartime memorials. Poignant reminders include Anne's first diary, her movie-star pin-up collection, height marks

Anne Frank Huis

left in pencil on the wall and original film footage. A separate wing focuses on rights and freedoms enjoyed today. Adm. Open 9am-9pm daily 1 Apr-31 Oct, 9am-7pm 1 Nov-31 Mar. Prinsengracht 263, T: 020 556 7100, www.annefrank.org

Artis Zoo ❶ 4G

Artis's multiple attractions include 6,000 animals, gardens with lakes and rambles, two museums (zoology and geology), a planetarium and a children's zoo where kids can meet the gentler creatures face to face. Founded in 1838, the zoo combines 19th-century ambience with a 21st-century approach: zebras, gazelles and giraffe inhabit an authentic African savannah, and the world-famous Aquarium

Gabled buildings in the Begijnhof

includes a section of transparent Amsterdam canal. *Adm. Open 9am-5pm daily 1 Nov-31 Mar, 9am-6pm 1 Apr-31 Oct, until sunset Sat Jun-Aug. Plantage Kerklaan 38-40, T: 020 523 3400, www.artis.nl*

Begijnhof ❷ 6A
Serene, secluded and pristine, the Begijnhof is a pocket of calm in the very heart of Amsterdam's bustling city centre. The grass-filled courtyard surrounded by tall, gabled houses was founded in the 14th century as a haven for *beguines*; these were unmarried women who had chosen to live a semi-monastic life but without formal vows. Standing out from the 18th-century buildings around it is *Het Houten Huys* (The Wooden House) made from wood in 1477 and Amsterdam's oldest building. The gothic 'English' church opposite the little house originally belonged to the *beguines*, but was taken over by English Protestants in the Reformation (some of whom went on to form the core group of America's Pilgrim Fathers). *Open 9am-5pm daily for individual visits, www.begijnhofamsterdam.nl*

Bloemenmarkt ❷ 7B
Amsterdam's floating flower market, dating back to 1862, is as beautiful and fragrant as ever, and spills out on to the quayside. Sadly these days the cut flowers and plants are all transported into town by lorry instead of the traditional boats wending their way through the canal system. Snap up unbeatable bargains on 2,700 varieties of tulips, bulbs of all kinds, geraniums, indoor cypresses, Christmas trees and 'mano' bulbs from Easter Island (please note that bulbs taken to the

US and Canada will need a health certificate). *Open 9.30am-5.30pm Mon-Sat, 11am-5pm Sun. Singel, bet Muntplein & Koningsplein.*

The Canal Ring
You could spend all day exploring the tree-lined canals along Amsterdam's dream-like Grachtengordel or 'Canal Ring'. The beautiful but spindly 17th-century mansions on Herengracht, Keizersgracht and Prinsengracht were built for wealthy merchants, bankers and politicians and taxed for

> ### The Narrowest House in the World
> One metre (3 ft) wide and just a few centimetres bigger than its front door, Amsterdam's narrowest house is at *Singel 7* ❷ 1B (behind closed doors the house widens to more normal proportions). *Oude Hoogstraat 22,* ❷ 5D, the city's smallest house, is a mere 2.2 metres (7 ft) wide and 6 metres (20 ft) deep.

Instantly recognisable lines of the EYE film museum

width – look out for all kinds of curious and elaborate decorations, from sphinxes, swags and busts to stupendously beautiful rooftop gables. Famous façades dominate the 'Golden Bend' on Herengracht between Leidsestraat and Vijzelstraat (❶ 5C), the Huis met de Hoofden (❶ 2C) with its Roman gods and goddess busts, and the romantic Magere Brug drawbridge (❶ 5E), illuminated at night with necklaces of light. (*See p.47 for tours by boat.*)

EYE Off map at ❶ 1F
Amsterdam's spectacular film museum sits on the north bank of the River IJ (a free ferry service runs 24/7 from Centraal Station, taking two minutes). The building is an architectural wonder housing four film auditoriums and offering panoramic views of the city. EYE's collection (over 37,000 films) is constantly expanding, containing silent films from the beginning of cinema, right through to the latest digital productions. The Basement is where visitors can browse the collection in the Panorama space, enter a Pod with its comfy sofa and Cinemascope screen for a more personal viewing experience, or engage with the interactive Installations in the Playground. *Adm. Basement open 10am-6pm daily. IJpromenade 1, T: 020 589 1400, www.eyefilm.nl*

Het Scheepvaartmuseum ❶ 3G

This mammoth, Venetian-style 17th-century warehouse houses a stupendous maritime museum, bursting at the gunnels with ships' models, figureheads and royal barges, maps and racing boats. Recently re-opened after extensive modernisation, visitors can experience a virtual 'Voyage at Sea', along with a host of interactive exhibitions. *Adm. Open 9am-5pm daily. Kattenburgerplein 1, T: 020 523 2222, www.hetscheepvaartmuseum.nl*

House of Bols ❶ 7B

The award-winning House of Bols Cocktail and Genever Experience offers a unique insight into the world of cocktails and liqueurs. The tour

Het Scheepvaartmuseum

starts in the Hall of Taste, introduces visitors to the World of Cocktails club, journeys through the mysterious Bols Genever (Dutch cocktail spirit dating back to 1820) Room and finishes in the Mirror Bar where you can try your hand at mixing cocktails in the Flair Booth. En route visitors will have all five senses engaged while learning about Lucas Bols, the word's oldest distilled spirit. Minimum age 18 years. *Adm. Open 12noon-6.30pm Sun-Thu, 12noon-10pm Fri, 12noon-8pm Sat. Paulus Potterstraat 14, T: 020 570 8575, www.bols.com*

Joods Historisch Museum ❷ 7F

Based in four 17th- and 18th-century Ashkenazi synagogues, the Jewish Historical Museum throws light on every aspect of the Jewish experience in Amsterdam, from the first Sephardic Jews who arrived from Portugal and Spain in 1600 to powerful accounts of WWII, when 100,000 Amsterdammers died in concentration camps. The museum also organises walks around the Jewish quarter and visits to the nearby Portuguese Synagogue (❷ 7F), which was the largest in

Learn your Gables

Simple spout gables as seen in (A) appeared in the 14th and 15th centuries, and they then became more ornate to disguise the steepness of the roofs behind them. Step gables (B) were popular in the 17th century, with neck gables (C) appearing between 1640 and 1840. Decorative bell gables (D) date from the 18th century.

True Brews

The famous Heineken Brewery tour – ending with an all-you-can-glug knees-up – is one of Amsterdam's greatest attractions (**1** 7C, *open 11am-7.30pm Mon-Thu, 11am-8.30pm Fri-Sun (last tickets 2 hrs before closing), Stadhouderskade 78, T: 020 523 9666, www.heinekenexperience. com*). For another beery brew, tour the microbrewery Brouwerij 't IJ, which produces 180,000 litres per year of malty *pils* from the Molen de Gooyer (**1** 3H), an 18th-century windmill. *Open 3pm-8pm Wed-Sun, English speaking tours 3.30pm Fri-Sun. Funenkade 7, T: 020 622 8325, www.brouwerijhetij.nl*

Europe when it was built in 1675. *Adm. Open 11am-5pm daily. Closed on Jewish holidays. Nieuwe Amstelstraat 1, T: 020 531 0310, www.jhm.nl*

Jordaan **1** 3A

Home to thousands of canal builders, stonemasons, stevedores and tradesmen since the 17th century, Amsterdam's oldest working-class district is now its coolest downtown neighbourhood. Come here by day and night for quirky off-beat shops and small experimental art galleries, for quintessential brown bars and laid-back lounges, for tapas bars and Thai restaurants, and, at Elandsgracht and Noorderkerk, for Amsterdam's best junk, antiques, flea and farmers' markets (De Looier, Noordermarkt and Rommelmarkt, *see pp.17, 21 & 58*). Some of the city's prettiest *hofjes* – almshouses with peaceful inner courtyards built in the 17th and 18th centuries for widows and the poor and elderly – are clustered here: including Suyckerhofje at *Lindengracht 149* and the Claes Claeshofje at *1e Egelantiersdwarsstraat 3*.

Koninklijk Paleis **2** 3B

Built on 13,659 wooden piles (a figure every Dutch child knows by heart), Jacob van Campen's city hall is a great masterpiece of Dutch Renaissance architecture. Don't miss its awesomely beautiful interior with its orgy of marble, bronze and sculpture (nibbling rats in the bankruptcy chamber; thunderbolts, skulls and snakes in the Court of Justice). In 1808 Napoleon's brother turned the building into a royal palace, complete with chandeliers and Empire furniture – the building is now owned by the state, but still

Amsterdam has:
About 1.5 million inhabitants, 600,000 flower bulbs, 600,000 bikes, 150,000 bike thefts a year, 2,500 houseboats, 1,402 bars and cafés, 206 Van Goghs, 165 canals (15 more than Venice), 22 Rembrandts, 26 markets, eight wooden drawbridges and six 17th- and 18th-century windmills.

occasionally plays host to royal functions and events, when it is closed to the public. *Adm. Open 11am-5pm (days vary); free tours in Dutch and English available on request (2 weeks' notice required), T: 020 620 4060, www.paleisamsterdam.nl*

NEMO ❶ 2G
NewMetropolis brings science and technology to life interactively: discover how an engine works, build a dam or make abominable smells in the working laboratory. Even more amazing is the building itself – a pale green ocean liner crashing into the river IJ by Pompidou architect Renzo Piano: the roof, with its views across the harbour, is free to visit. *Adm. Open 10am-5pm Tue-Sun Sep-May, daily Jun-Aug. Oosterdok 2, T: 020 531 3233, www.e-nemo.nl*

Ons' Lieve Heer op Solder ❷ 2D
Resembling paintings by Vermeer, the intricate interiors of this stunning museum evoke the Golden Age more powerfully than anywhere else in Amsterdam. A succession of exquisite period rooms culminates in the tiny

Nemo, designed by Italian architect Renzo Piano

but spectacular secret upstairs chapel dedicated to *Ons' Lieve Heer op Solder* (*Our Dear Lord in the Attic*). Including an altarpiece painting by Jacob de Wit, the sumptuous chapel was one of 30 or so 'hidden' churches used from 1680-1795, when Catholics were banned from worshipping in public. *Adm. Open Mon-Sat 10am-5pm, 1pm-5pm Sun and hols. Oudezijds Voorburgwal 40, T: 020 624 6604, www.opsolder.nl*

Rembrandthuis ❷ 6E
Rembrandt's home from 1639-1658 gives mesmerising glimpses into the genius's life, from the kitchen with its ornate box-bed and courtyard where he painted *The Night Watch* to print rooms, studios and a cabinet of curiosities with shells, bones, weapons, stuffed animals and globes contained in his actual paintings. A gallery wing shows highlights from the museum's unique collection of

Rijksmuseum interior

more than 250 Rembrandt etchings, along with impressive changing exhibitions. Adm. Open 10am-6pm daily. Jodenbreestraat 4, T: 020 520 0400, www.rembrandthuis.nl

Rijksmuseum ❶ 6B

After a ten year programme of renovation and modernisation costing over €333m, the Rijksmuseum finally re-opened its doors to the general public in April 2013. The building itself is a neo-Gothic extravaganza designed in 1885 by Pierre Cuypers. Architects have painstakingly stripped the building of its later additions to reveal Cuypers' original design and layout and have restored the opulent decorations to their former glory. State-of-the-art additions such as climate-control and high-tech security features now ensure the preservation of the museum's world-class art collection housed within this magnificent building. Highlights include 'The Masterpieces' featuring works from the Golden Age. Visitors will also find Rembrandt's *Night Watch* on display, along with Vermeer's *Milkmaid*. The collection is extensive, with over 400 pieces of art and historical artifacts for art lovers to enjoy. Adm. Open 9am-5pm daily. Museumstraat 1, T: 020 674 7000, www.rijksmuseum.nl

Stedelijk Museum ❶ 7A

The late 19th-century building housing the largest collection of modern and contemporary art and design in the Netherlands underwent a recent modernization programme resulting in a futuristic extension. Key works by Matisse, Kandinsky and Jackson Pollock are on display, along with extensive design collections incorporating furniture, glass, ceramics and print. Dynamic and imaginative exhibitions are guaranteed. *Adm. Open 10am-6pm Fri-Wed, 10am-10pm Thu. Museumplein 10, T: 020 573 2911, www.stedelijk.nl*

Stedelijk Museum

Tropenmuseum & Kindermuseum ❶ 5H
This superb anthropological museum is unique in Europe. Stroll through the courtyard of a peasant house in Java, explore a noisy Arab streetmarket or experience a violent thunderstorm in the African savannah. As well as exhibits of stunning artefacts, the museum has a tropical-themed shop and restaurant, plus the award-winning Kindermuseum for kids aged 6-12, which evokes a wealth of different cultures with singing, storytelling and theatre. *Adm. Open 10am-5pm daily. Linnaeusstraat 2, T: 020 568 8200, www.tropenmuseum.nl*

Van Gogh Museum ❶ 7B
This houses one of the world's most sensational art collections – 200 amazing paintings, 580 drawings and 850 letters penned by Vincent Van Gogh, presented in a

> ### Passion-o-ramas
> Take in 15 bridges in one go (including the one you're standing on) from the bridge at Reguliersgracht and Herengracht – best at night, when the arches are illuminated with hundreds of lights. For other stunning panoramas, head for the top-floor restaurant of Metz & Co (*see p.18*), the roof of the NEMO (*see p.9*) or the 17th-century towers of the Zuiderkerk (❷ 5E) and the Westerkerk (*see p.12*).

stunningly beautiful light-filled gallery space designed by Dutch architect Gerrit Rietveld. A Zen-like water sculpture links Rietveld's 1973 building to the awesomely minimalist temporary exhibitions gallery, which was designed by Japanese architect Kisho Kurokawa in 1999 (and financed by the same Japanese insurance company that paid £35m for Van Gogh's *Sunflowers* in 1987). *Adm.* Open 9am-6pm daily 1 May- 1 Sep, 9am-5pm 2 Sep-30 Apr, 10am-10pm Fri. Closed 1 Jan. *Paulus Potterstraat 7, T: 020 570 5200, www.vangoghmuseum.nl*

Vondelpark ❶ 6A
Laid out in the 19th century with rambles, lakes and lawns, Vondelpark is still the ultimate summertime hangout. Places to preen and be seen include free gigs and concerts at the open-air theatre, tea at the classic 1930s Round Blue Teahouse and cocktails and dinner at the historic Pavilion's restaurant, Vertigo (dining on the terrace in the evening is a sublime experience).

Westerkerk Tower ❶ 2B
It's a 186-step climb up Hendrick de Keyser's magnificent tower, but worth it for the fabulous views from the top. Amsterdam's most beautiful

View the sensational art collection at the Van Gogh Museum

Amsterdam for Free
The Dutch are a generous nation and you could spend a week visiting Amsterdam's free sights: top spots include the Civic Guards Gallery, Begijnhof (*see p.5*), Rijksmuseum garden (*see p.10*), Concertgebouw lunchtime concerts (*see p.24*), Bloemenmarkt's floating flowers (*see pp.5, 20*), and free ferries across the IJ river (ferries to the north side of the city leave 24 hours a day: go to landing-stage Seven (❶ 1E, behind Centraal Station).

Relaxing in Vondelpark

Westerkerk Tower

Protestant church was finished in 1631, nine years after De Keyser's death (Rembrandt and his son were buried here in unmarked paupers' graves). With its two 17th-century organs, the cavernous interior makes the perfect venue for Bach cantata concerts. *Tower open 10am-5pm Mon-Sat Apr-Sep. Prinsengracht 281, T: 020 624 7766, www.westerkerk.nl*

Willet-Holthuysen Museum ❶ 5E

Catch a glimpse of the sybaritic lifestyle of Amsterdam's 18th-century merchant classes at this perfectly restored canal house including an exquisite Meissen dinner service in the dining room. Tours can be arranged on request. *Adm. Open 10am-5pm Mon-Fri, 11am-5pm Sat-Sun and hols. Herengracht 605, T: 020 523 1822, www.willetholthuysen.nl*

amsterdam places to shop

With some of the best markets, small shops and boutiques in the world, Amsterdam's a place to rummage, browse and cool-hunt. Tucked away on its side streets, canals and squares are an incredible 10,400 shops, 141 cutting-edge art galleries and 22 flower, food and flea markets. Whether it's toys or teapots, kites or condoms, edgy avant-garde haute couture or museum-quality antiques, Amsterdam has an outlet catering to every predilection. For seriously decadent shopping sprees, start early in the morning at the markets, trawl the city centre (Dam Square, Kalverstraat, Leidsestraat) for department stores and club-wear cool, then hit 'Nine Streets' and the Jordaan for a mixed bag of delectable collectibles and fashionista chic.

buy it places to shop

Areas

Damstraat-Hoogstraat ❷ 4D-5E

Bordering the Red Light District: full of shops stuffed with drugs paraphernalia but worth visiting for funky clubwear, second-hand bookshops and offbeat boutiques.

Haarlemmerbuurt

So hip it's off-map, this upcoming barrio north of Jordaan is home to the Westergasfabriek (see p.27) arts-complex and a smattering of choice and quirky boutiques and cafés.

'Nine Streets' at sunset

Jordaan ❶ 3A

A paradise of young designer boutiques, quirky art galleries, antiques and junk shops plus some of the city's most enticing food stores, bakeries and markets.

Nieuwedijk-Kalverstraat ❷ 1C-7B

Amsterdam's busiest shopping streets: pedestrianised, packed with people and prime hunting territory for some amazing bargains on high-street brand names.

'Nine Streets' ❶ 3B

The shop-nirvana of narrow streets crisscrossing picturesque Prinsengracht and Herengracht is crammed with hundreds of delectable boutiques, gourmet delis, hip cafés and cool speciality stores.

P. C. Hooftstraat-Van Baerlestraat ❶ 6A-6B

Near the museums and Amsterdam's flashiest shopping nexus, chock full of chichi designer emporia and exclusive interior design stores.

Spiegelkwartier ❶ 5C

High-quality antiques and art: stratospheric prices but worth a go-see for some razzle-dazzle window-shopping.

Utrechtsestraat ❶ 5D

Ultra elegant shopping and restaurant hotspot: stylish and eclectic luxury fashion, shoe design, modern furniture and gourmet speciality shops.

Antiques & Auction Houses

The Antique Ring Shop ❷ 6D
Previously called Charel Antiques but now specialising in antique jewellery. An extensive collection of exquisite rings from a bygone era. *Open 11am-6pm Tue-Sat, 1pm-5pm Sun. Staalstraat 18, T: 020 689 3214, www.antiqueringshop.com*

De Looier Antiekcentrum ❶ 4A
With 72 stands, several bigger shops, a café and 90 display cabinets, this is a labyrinthine market offering antiques, art and collectibles of varying quality for sale. *Open 11am-6pm Mon and Wed-Fri, 11am- 5pm Sat-Sun. Elandsgracht 109, T: 020 624 9038, www.antiekcentrumamsterdam.com*

Eduard Kramer ❶ 5C
Exquisite, hand-painted antique Delft floor and wall tiles, period jewellery, candelabra and decanters. *Open 1pm-6pm Sun-Mon, 10am-6pm Tue-Sat. Nieuwe Spiegelstraat 64, T: 020 623 0832, www.antique-tileshop.nl*

Art Galleries

Fons Welters ❶ 2A
Big-name Dutch artists, with an emphasis on expensive sculpture and conceptual art. *Bloemstraat 140, T: 020 423 3046, www.fonswelters.nl*

Radar Architecture and Art ❶ 2A
Founded by architect Marco di Piaggi, this independent gallery embraces the avant-garde. *Open 1pm-5pm Fri-Sat. Rozengracht 77A, www.radar-amsterdam.com*

Serieuze Zaken Studioos Off map
Rob Malasch's seriously meaty mix of contemporary art from home and abroad, including BritArt. *Postjesweg 2, T: 020 427 5770, www.serieuzezaken.info*

Beer

De Bierkoning ❷ 4A
950 kinds of beer from around the world, with 300 different glasses to go with them. Helpful advice on Dutch specialities such as *Zatte*, a bottle-fermented beer. *Paleisstraat 125, T: 020 625 2336, www.bierkoning.nl*

Books

American Book Center ❷ 6A
Huge selection of US and UK books and magazines, on three floors with literary events held in their on-site treehouse. *Spui 12, T: 020 625 5537, www.abc.nl*

The English Bookshop ❶ 3A
Friendly, independent bookshop in the heart of the Jordaan. The onsite café is a recent addition and the ideal spot to relax with your latest purchase. They also offer writing workshops and a monthly English bookclub. *Open 11am-6pm Tue-Sat. Lauriergracht 71, T: 020 626 4230, www.englishbookshop.nl*

Oudenmanhuispoort Book Market ❷ 6C
A hidden gem and full of charm, nestled in a passageway between the old university buildings. Wide selection of second-hand books and sheet music. *Open Mon-Sat, Oudenmanhuispoort.*

Cheese

Henri Willig Kaas ❷ 1D
A fabulous array of cheeses, including free samples galore. Stay a while and watch the cheeses being made, before being served by the friendly female counter staff, all clad in traditional Dutch milkmaid costumes. *Haringpakkerssteeg 10-18, T: 020 624 1006, www.cheeseandmore.com*

Chocolate

Metropolitan Chocolate C.V. ❷ 3C
A mecca for those with a sweet tooth. Homemade gelato and freshly baked waffles, served with their very own chocolate, straight from the bean. *Warmoesstraat 135A, T: 020 330 1955, www.metropolitandeli.nl*

Clogs

Wooden Shoe Factory ❷ 5E
A vast array of traditional and contemporary clogs. *St Antonies-breestraat 39-51, T: 020 427 3862, www.woodenshoefactory.com*

People really do buy clogs ...

Department Stores

De Bijenkorf ❷ 3C
Bold and brassy, this is Amsterdam's biggest store, covering five floors; with everything you could ever want, from linens, household goods and chic designer kitchenware to cosmetics and designer clothes, including hipsters' club- and streetwear. *Dam 1, T: 020 621 8080, www.bijenkorf.nl*

Maison de Bonneterie ❷ 6B
Oh-so-snootily, icily posh, dripping chandeliers, top designer labels, and exquisite bed and bathroom linens. All in the best possible taste. *Rokin 140-142, T: 020 531 3400, www.debonneterie.nl*

Metz & Co ❶ 5C
Style heaven: from slick and decorative designer fashion to furnishings, fabrics and homeware to die for. Don't miss the top-floor café with its stunning views across the city. *Leidsestraat 34-36, T: 020 520 7020, www.metz-co.nl*

Diamonds

Coster Diamonds ❶ 6B
Reputable diamond dealer, cutter and polisher. *Paulus Potterstraat 2-6, T: 020 305 5555, www.costerdiamonds.com*

Gassan Diamonds ❷ 5F
A visit to the steam-driven 400-year-old diamond factory that Gassan now reside in is an experience not to be

missed. Learn about the craftsmanship involved in producing the Amsterdam Cut, before having the opportunity to buy at the end of the tour. *Open 9am-5pm daily. Nieuwe Uilenburgerstraat 175, T: 020 622 5333, www.gassan.com*

Fashion

Cora Kemperman ❶ 5B
Avant-garde layered creations by the vanguard Dutch designer.
Leidsestraat 72, T: 020 625 1284, www.corakemperman.nl

Lock Stock & Barrel ❶ 3B
Founded by Mare and Elza in 2006, this independent boutique presents an eclectic collection of individually sourced luxury pieces from around the world. *Hartenstraat 26, T: 020 421 3348, www.lockstockbarrel.nl*

Household

Capsicum ❷ 5D
Wondrous fabrics to choose from, with classical music playing.
Oude Hoogstraat 1, T: 020 623 1016, www.capsicum.nl

Frozen Fountain ❶ 4B
Avant-garde contemporary furniture, ceramics, fabrics and jewellery; with an annual exhibition featuring work by upcoming design graduates. *Prinsengracht 645, T: 020 622 9375, www.frozenfountain.com*

Kitsch Kitchen ❶ 2B
Colourful kitsch and 1950s nostalgia for the discerning cook, as well as party goods, stationery, kooky gifts for toddlers, trendy shopping bags and umbrellas, and retro housewares. *Rozengracht 8-12, T: 020 462 0051, www.kitschkitchen.nl*

Hubble Bubble

Dampkring ❶ 1D
Seeds, including skunk, for cultivation, bulbs, pipes and hydroponic growing equipment.

De Bijenkorf, Amsterdam's biggest department store

Prins Hendrikkade 10-11,
www.dampkring.nl

Lingerie

Hunkemöller ❷ 6B
Trendy and feminine underwear for
all sizes. *Kalverstraat 162,
T: 020 623 6032, www.hunkemoller.com*

Salon de Lingerie ❶ 5D
Expensive, glamorous lingerie.
*Utrechtsestraat 38, T: 020 623 9857,
www.salondelingerie.nl*

Tax-Free Amsterdam
Non-EU residents can save
19 per cent on single
purchases exceeding €50: ask
for an export certificate at the
till and have it stamped at
customs when you leave.
Shops with 'Tax-free for
Tourists' signs issue tax-free
Global Refund Cheques, which
can be cashed in at Schiphol
Airport or refunded by credit
card. *www.easytaxfree.com*

Mall

Magna Plaza ❷ 3A
All streaky-bacon brickwork and neo-
Gothic pinnacles, Amsterdam's
amazing 1899 Postkantoor (Head
Post Office) is one of the city's
architectural gems. In the 1990s the
entire building was sleekly converted
into a mammoth shopping complex,
with 40 arcaded retail outlets for
jeans, jewels, toys and fashion.

Delicate brickwork façade of Magna Plaza

Nieuwezijds Voorburgwal 182, T: 020
570 3570, www.magnaplaza.nl

Markets

Amsterdam has 26 historic markets,
each with its keynote atmosphere.

Albert Cuypmarkt ❶ 7D
Noisy and sprawling, with nearly
300 stalls selling food, fabrics and
T-shirts: check out the cheese stalls
and Indonesian and Middle Eastern
street-food. *Open 9am-5pm Mon-Sat.
Albert Cuypstraat,
www.albertcuypmarkt.nl*

Bloemenmarkt ❷ 7B
Huge and colourful plant and flower
market on the Singel canal, with
floating stalls (see p.5). *Open
9am-5.30pm Mon-Sat, 11am-5.30pm
Sun. Singel.*

IJ Hallen Off map
Europe's largest flea market held over
one weekend, every month. Free ferry
from behind Centraal Station to
NDSM Wharf. *Check website for dates.
Neveritaweg 15, www.ij-hallen.nl*

Kunstmarkt ❷ 6A
High-quality art market. *Open 10am-3pm Sun. Spui, Thorbeckeplein.*

Noordermarkt ❶ 1B
Vintage paraphernalia from books to jewellery, with a luscious farmers' produce market (*boerenmarkt*) on Sat. *Open 9am-2pm Mon, 9am-5pm Sat. Noordermarkt.*

Waterlooplein ❷ 6E
Bulging at the seams with vintage leather jackets, denim and clubwear, jewellery and junk; touristy but fun. Watch out for pickpockets. *Open 9am-6pm, Mon-Sat. Waterlooplein.*

Secondhand & Vintage Clothing

Wini ❶ 1D
From vintage Chanel to the bohemian 1960s and psychedelic 1970s, Wini stocks an impressive range of retro clothing, shoes, trinkets and accessories. *Haarlemmerstraat 29, T: 020 427 9393, www.winivintage.nl*

Speciality Shops

Concerto ❶ 5E
The vinyl and CD scene is alive and kicking in Amsterdam, with Concerto's gradual extension to cover five shop fronts providing all the evidence you need. Nothing flashy, just row upon row of music in all formats. A music lover's idea of heaven. *Utrechtsestraat 52-60, T: 020 623 5228, www.concerto.nl*

Condomerie Het Gulden Vlies ❷ 3C
A longstanding and well known Amsterdam destination on the edge of the Red Light District; condoms of every size, shape, colour and flavour. They also offer safe sex and condom workshops. *Warmoesstraat 141, T: 020 627 4174 , www.condomerie.com*

Conscious Dreams Kokopelli ❶ 2D
The spectrum of smart shop psychedelia: magic mushrooms, psycho-active cacti, herbal ecstasies, aphrodisiacs and plants. *Warmoesstraat 12, T: 020 421 7000, www.consciousdreams.nl*

Winkel (Shop) Opening Times
Normal shop opening hours are 1pm-6pm Monday, 9am-6pm Tuesday-Friday and 9am-5pm Saturday. Most shops (*winkels*) close on Monday mornings and stay open as late as 9pm on Thursday; larger shops and stores are open 12noon-5pm Sunday.

Deksels Off map
The ultimate in chic kitchen utensils and accessories. *Open 11am-6pm Wed-Sat. Haarlemmerdijk 129, T: 020 528 9613, www.deksels-amsterdam.nl*

P.G.C. Hajenius ❷ 5B
The smoker's shop of shops, with an Art Deco interior and the best cigars in town. *Rokin 96, T: 020 623 7494, www.hajenius.com*

Stout ❶ 3B
Tasteful erotica. *Berenstraat 9, T: 020 620 1676, www.stoutinternational.com*

amsterdam entertainment

Amsterdam's clubs, jazz bars, cinemas, dance studios, concert halls and theatres are hives of hectic night-time activity. An exuberant cultural vibe embraces the flawless Concertgebouw, high-camp film-fests, Stockhausen premieres and progressive drum 'n' bass. Arts subsidies keep highbrow venues affordable and in the summer hundreds of open-air concerts and spectaculars are staged for free. For the spectrum of upcoming events, scrutinise websites, newspapers and magazines, especially *Amsterdam Weekly* (online at *www.amsterdamweekly.nl*), AUB's *Uitkrant* and *Time Out*'s monthly online listings at *www.timeout.com/amsterdam*

watch it entertainment

Cinema

Foreign films are shown in their original language with subtitles in Dutch (often with a 15-minute intermission mid-way). To find out what's on, check the free listings agendas in cinemas, bars and cafés or see www.filmladder.nl To reserve in advance T: 0900 9363 (Dutch language only). Also check out the EYE film museum (see p.6).

Pathe de Munt ❶ 5D

Pathe are the largest chain of cinemas in the Netherlands. This particular one is centrally located and offers all the latest releases. Films are often screened in English with Dutch subtitles. Vijzelstraat 15, T: 0900 1458, www.pathe.nl

Pathé Tuschinski ❷ 7C

Amsterdam's Art Deco tour de force is a sight in itself: take a free guided tour by day (Sun/Mon, by appointment) or splash out on a luxurious box and champagne at night (late programmes include live mime and tap dancing shows). Reguliersbreestraat 26-28, T: 0900 1458, www.pathe.nl

The Movies Off map

Fabulous palace dating from 1928, showing arthouse and mainstream movies until late; with a restaurant and café. Haarlemmerdijk 161, T: 020 638 6016, www.themovies.nl

Classical & Opera

Home to Mariss Jansons' matchless Royal Concertgebouw, Amsterdam is also a world-ranked showcase for early and contemporary music. For programmes, check the free listings magazines Uitkrant (www.uitlijn.nl) and Shark (www.underwateramsterdam.com); reserve tickets at AUB or the tourist board (see box Tickets Please, p.30).

Concertgebouw ❶ 7A

The jewel in the crown of Amsterdam's classical music scene, with regular performances by top international players and orchestras. During summer months there are Sunday morning concerts at 11am and free Wednesday lunch concerts

Carry-on Carillon
Don't miss the church-bell carillons built by the Hemony brothers in the 17th century. Catch an hour-long concert:
Munttoren (❷ 7B, see pic left), Fri at noon.
Oude Kerk (❷ 3D, see right) Sat at 4pm.
Westerkerk (❶ 2B, see p.13) Tue at 12noon.
Zuiderkerk (❷ 5E) Thu at 12noon.

Concertgebouw frontage

at 12.30pm. A guided tour (in English) of the complex is offered on Sunday at noon and on Monday at 5pm. *Concertgebouwplein 2-6, T: 020 671 8345, www.concertgebouw.nl*

Het Muziektheater ❷ 7E
Dubbed the 'Stopera' when it was built in the 1980s, the controversial city hall (Stadhuis) and opera house complex is HQ of the highly acclaimed Nederlands Opera. *Amstel 3, T: 020 625 5455, www.muziektheater.nl*

Muziekgebouw aan 't IJ ❶ 1G
This 21st-century music complex houses Amsterdam's acoustically brilliant auditorium for new music, as well as the new location of the city's venerable jazz club, the Bimhuis. The Star Ferry, on the ground floor, has a restaurant and outdoor terrace with one of the most spectacular views in town. *Piet Heinkade 1. T: 020 788 2000 (box office), www.het-muziektheater.nl*

Oude Kerk ❷ 3D
Organ, chamber music, choral and carillon recitals. Also organises a summer 'walking concert' series. *Oudekerksplein 23, T: 020 625 8284, www.oudekerk.nl*

Clubs

To find out what's hot and what's not, pick up flyers and freebies from happening bars and cafés, or shops. Clubs range from exclusive (for that, read expensive) to laid-back and affordable; remember to tip the bouncer €1-2 (and to keep some change back for the toilets).

Bitterzoet ❷ 1C
Amsterdam's avant-garde artists hang out in this performance venue that's a mix of club with DJs, bar, cutting-edge theatre and occasional

> **Culture Vulture**
> From June to August, Vondelpark holds free pop, jazz, theatre and opera performances at the Open-Air Theatre. *Vondelpark Openluchttheater, T: 020 673 1499, www.openluchttheater.nl*

Oude Kerk organ

25

cinema. *Open till 4am weekends.*
Spuistraat 2, T: 020 421 2318,
www.bitterzoet.com

Club Up ❶ 5B

A colourful mix of dance-loving
hipsters congregate nightly to chill in
the hidden mezzanine and throw
some shapes on the vast dance floor
below. Cocktails flow and funky beats
resonate until the small hours. *Korte
Leidsedwarsstraat 26, T: 020 623 6985,
www.clubup.nl*

Escape ❷ 7D

Amsterdam's largest and sweatiest
dance venue in a converted cinema,
with room for 2,000 clubbers.
A steady stream of internationally
renowned DJs have been known to
grace the decks, while the most
popular weekly club nights are
'Reveal' on a Thursday and 'Frame
Busters' house music party on a
Saturday. *Rembrandtplein 11, T: 020
622 1111, www.escape.nl*

Panama Off map at ❶ 1H

Housed in an old power station in the
docks east of Centraal Station,
Panama gets going with live music
at about 9pm, and then a host of
DJs take you through the night.
Restaurant and popular terrace bar.
*Oostelijke Handelskade 4, T: 020 311
8686, www.panama.nl*

Studio 80 ❶ 4D

A non-stop party vibe created by a
stream of techno DJs, both local and
international, keep the crowds
satisfied. The décor is sparse, but
with a capacity for 300 the dance
floor is usually jumping.
Rembrandtplein 17, www.studio-80.nl

Dance

Many top international
choreographers work with the two
home-grown international ballet
companies; smaller venues bristle
with interesting work by folk, jazz
and experimental dance groups.

Het Internationaal
Danstheater ❷ 6D

Features folk and world dance
performances directed by famous
guest choreographers.
*Kloveniersburgwal 87, T: 020 623 9112,
www.intdanstheater.nl*

Het Muziektheater ❷ 7E
(see also p.25)

Home to the Dutch National
Ballet (with a repertoire ranging
from 19th-century classics to
contemporary), the Muziektheater
also showcases work by visiting

Het Muziektheater is nicknamed 'Stopera'

companies. Capacity is 1,600. *Box Office: T: 020 551 8225. Amstel 3, T: 020 625 5455, www.het-ballet.nl*

Jazz & Salsa

Amsterdam is considered to be one of Europe's finest jazz venues, representing every kind of style from blues and Dixie to avant-garde. To find out who's playing when and at which venues, visit the all-knowing 'what's on' website at *www.amsterdamsuitburo.nl*, or drop by the AUB (*see box Tickets Please, p.30*). There are jazz performances held in Vondelpark during the summer (*see box Culture Vulture, p.25*).

Bimhuis ❶ 1G
Mingus, Sun Ra and Art Blakey have all performed at this legendary hotspot, which puts on more than 250 concerts each year at its new waterfront location. *Piet Heinkade 3, T: 020 788 2188, www.bimhuis.nl*

Bourbon Street ❶ 5B
Laid-back bar with jazz and blues performed till 3am. *Leidsekruisstraat 6-8, Leidseplein, T: 020 623 3440, www.bourbonstreet.nl*

Jazz Café Alto ❶ 5B
Small café offering a meaty menu of jazz and blues. This place is so popular, it's packed out most nights. *Korte Leidsedwarsstraat 115, Leidseplein, T: 020 626 3249, www.jazz-cafe-alto.nl*

Gaming

Holland Casino Amsterdam ❶ 5B
This casino has lots to offer in addition to a roulette wheel. Cabarets are staged at 6.30pm from Wednesday to Sunday, there is a restaurant on the lower floor with a blissful waterside terrace, and an orchestra plays waltzes in the background. Passport required. *Max Euweplein 62, T: 020 521 1111, www.hollandcasino.nl*

Multimedia

Sugar Factory ❶ 5B
This popular 'night theatre' has seized a deserved place in

Westergasfabriek

Amsterdam's club scene. The mixed bag includes a range of performers in dance, jazz, spoken word and hip hop. The MCs are as unique as the acts. *Lijnbaansgracht 238. T: 020 627 0008, www.sugarfactory.nl*

Westergasfabriek Off map
Based in an awesome 19th-century gasworks and hosting a rich, eclectic and adventurous mix of theatre and dance, fashion, club and techno parties, pop concerts and classical music (Stockhausen's Helicopter String Quartet premiered here in 1995). With a dance-restaurant and film studios. *Polonceaukade 27, T: 020 586 0710, www.westergasfabriek.nl*

Picturesque canals and houses

Rock, Pop & World Music

Venues range from 50,000-seat stadiums and vanguard multimedia arts centres to clubs, cafés and Irish bars. For tickets to big events visit the AUB (see right, Tickets Please). To find out who's on, see posters and flyers or the English-language *Shark* magazine, online at *www.underwateramsterdam.com*

Akhnaton ❷ 2C

Small venue for heaving world music parties. *Nieuwezijds Kolk 25, T: 020 624 3396, www.akhnaton.nl*

Maloe Melo ❶ 3A

Sweaty and louche but still considered a cool musicians' hangout: performances include live music acts and blues, rock and jamming sessions. *Lijnbaansgracht 163, T: 020 420 4592, www.maloemelo.nl*

Melkweg ❶ 5B

A former dairy, the 'Milky Way' is now a cutting-edge multimedia arts venue for film and art as well as live

---

Lunchtime Freebies

Sneak a look at Amsterdam's sell-out classical concerts at the free lunchtime rehearsals at the Concertgebouw (see p.24) at 12.30pm-1pm Wednesday and at the Muziektheater (see p.25) at 12.15pm Tuesday.

---

gigs (there's also a popular and accessible dance night on Saturday and a trendy café-bar/restaurant). *Lijnbaansgracht 234a, T: 020 531 8181, www.melkweg.nl*

Paradiso ❶ 6B

This 'pop temple' is situated in an old church that the Rolling Stones have played at various stages of their career. Besides the main concert hall downstairs, which has hosted acts including Link Wray, The Sex Pistols, Nirvana, Patti Smith, Lily Allen and Cat Power, there is a smaller hall upstairs where upcoming artists are often showcased. Club events often follow concerts and go on until at least 4am. *Weteringschans 6-8, T: 020 626 4521, www.paradiso.nl*

The Waterhole ❶ 5B

It's dark and it's dingy and it's very definitely ready to rock seven nights a week. An old school rock bar. *Korte Leidsedwarsstraat 48, T: 020 620 8904, www.waterhole.nl*

Theatre

Options for English-language speakers include cabaret, stand-up, mime and touring productions.

Boom Chicago ❶ 3A

The in-house troupe puts on nightly shows that combine sharp writing, quick thinking and slick production. Many people come for dinner before

---

Tickets Please

Amsterdam Uitburo (AUB) sells tickets for concerts, opera, rock and pop gigs, theatre and other big events: visit their ticketshop at *Leidseplein 26*, or T: 0900 0191, *www.uitburo.nl* (Dutch language only).

Crowded dance floor at Paradiso

Sport

Climbing Wall

Klimhal Amsterdam Off map
Both indoor and outdoor climbing
opportunities for all ages, from
complete beginner to seasoned pro.
*Naritaweg 48, T: 020 681 0121,
www.klimhalamsterdam.nl*

Papageno statue at the Stadsschouwburg

the show. Drinks service continues
during the performance, which often
involves audience participation. Food
and drink packages available for
groups. *Rozengracht 117, T: 020 217
0400, www.boomchicago.nl*

Koninklijk Theater Carré ❶ 6E
Built in 1897 and a top venue for
highbrow touring productions,
musicals, cabaret, opera, ballet
and a Christmas circus.
*Amstel 115-125, T: 0900 2525 255,
www.theatercarre.nl*

De Kleine Komedie ❷ 7C
The city's oldest theatre, dating
back to 1788. Warm and
cosy, attracting some of the
Netherlands' finest talent.
*Amstel 56-58, T: 020 624 0534,
www.dekleinekomedie.nl*

Stadsschouwburg ❶ 5B
A 19th-century venue that has
dance performances and occasional
English shows in the Bovenzaal
upstairs. *Leidseplein 26,
T: 020 624 2311, www.ssba.nl*

watch it

Red Light Time

The Red Light District (❷ 3D), also known as 'De Wallen', with its mesmerising neon panoply of window-brothels, peep-shows and porn shops, has become a tired cliché for tourists looking for cheap thrills. In 2001 the brothels were regulated, with at least 5,000 prostitutes officially registered. In 2008, a campaign known as 'Postcode 1012' was generated by the city with the aim of drastically reducing the number of window prostitutes, gambling halls, coffee shops and seedy hotels in the area. More than a quarter of the windows have been shut down, some replaced by community art projects. The area from Centraal Station along the Damrak is a major target for a gentrification/beautification programme that has been long overdue.

Football

The demi-gods of Dutch football are Eindhoven's PSV and Amsterdam's own Ajax (pronounced 'i-axe') based at the Amsterdam Arena in the suburbs. Tickets to both are virtually impossible to get hold of.

Ajax Museum ❹

For daily World of Ajax tours (9am-6pm), visit *www.amsterdamarena.nl*. *Amsterdam Arena, Arena Boulevard 29, T: 020 311 1336/020 311 1444.*

Gym & Sauna

Splash Healthclub ❶ 5B

Total fitness facilities, day passes available. *Open 7am-12midnight Mon-Fri, 8am-9pm Sat-Sun. Lijnbaansgracht 241, T: 020 422 0280, www.splashamsterdam.nl*

Hockey

The season runs September-May and the top men's and women's teams play at: Wagener Stadium in Amstelveen, T: 030 751 3400, www.knhb.nl

Ajax are a national obsession

Horse Riding

De Amsterdamse Manege ❹

Supervised rides in the Amsterdamse Bos. The riding school offers indoor and outdoor lessons. Licensed bar for non-riders. *Nieuwe Kalfjeslaan 25, Amstelveen, T: 020 643 1342, www.deamsterdamsemanege.nl*

Ice-Skating

Whenever the ice is thick enough, Amsterdammers skate on the canals. There are ice rinks in Leidseplein and Museumplein, open in season, and surrounded by cafés and bars in which to warm up after a sojourn on the ice.

Jaap Eden (Off map)

Indoor rink and 400-m (1,312-ft) ice track. *Radioweg 64, Watersgraafsmeer, T: 0900 724 2287, www.jaapeden.nl*

Korfball

This strange-sounding sport is a fusion of netball, basketball and volleyball. Mixed teams play September-June at the Sportpark Joos Banckersweg, near Jan van Galenstraat, *www.knkv.nl*

Rollerblading

Amsterdammers love inline skating: Vondelpark hosts the weekly 15-km (nine-mile) Friday Night Skate, *www.fridaynightskate.com*

Rent-a-Skate ❶ 6A

Traditional and inline skates for hire. *Open Apr-Sep. Vondelpark 7, Amstelveenseweg entrance, T: 020 664 5091.*

Snooker

Club 8 Off map

Snooker and pool tables, attracting all levels of player. *Admiraal de Ruijterweg 56B, T: 020 685 1703, www.club-8.nl*

Swimming

Zuiderbad ❶ 7B

Beautiful swimming pool dating from 1912, with nude bathing allowed Sunday 4.30pm-5.30pm. *Hobbemastraat 26, T: 020 252 1390, www.zuid.amsterdam.nl*

Ten-Pin Bowling

Knijn Bowling Centre ❹

Opposite the RAI; 18 lanes and a disco Friday and Saturday till 1am. There's also a restaurant here. *Scheldeplein 3, Zuid, T: 020 664 2211, www.knijnbowling.nl*

Skating all winter on Museumplein

amsterdam places to eat and drink

Wherever you go in Amsterdam, you're never far from food. Lunch can be a hand-held feast, eaten in the street and selected from a range of tempting exotica, including fries dipped in mayonnaise, spicy saté chicken, falafel, filled rolls (*belegde broodje*), raw herring (the local speciality) or waffles, pancakes and Dutch apple pie. For something more substantial, brown bars and *eetcafés* provide a cosy backdrop for a mixed bag of hearty Dutch fare (pea soup or ham and fried eggs on bread) and more adventurous restaurant-quality cooking. In the evening, splash out on an Indonesian *rijsttafel* (a Dutch-colonial 'rice table' feast of as many as 20 hot and spicy dishes) or top-notch nosh in Michelin-starred La Rive.

taste it places to eat and drink

Price **per person**
€ = cheap < €10
€€ = moderate €10-35
€€€ = expensive > €35

Classic Dutch

Brasserie Keyzer €€ ❶ 7A

This musicians' mecca is next door to the Concertgebouw (see p.24) and has been serving classic food since 1903. *Van Baerlestraat 96, Museum Quarter, T: 020 675 1866, www.brasseriekeyzer.nl*

d'Vijff Vlieghen €€€ ❶ 3C

Traditional Dutch cooking with local, seasonal, organic ingredients. The

Brasserie Keyzer

classical 17th-century ambience contributes to an unforgettable dining experience. *Spuistraat 294, T: 020 530 4060.*

Moeders €€ ❶ 3A

On opening night (1990) guests were asked to bring their own crockery; these are still used by diners today. A charming spot to sample traditional Dutch dishes under the watchful gaze of the mothers (*moeders*) whose pictures adorn the walls. *Rozengracht 251, T: 020 626 7957, www.moeders.com*

Restaurant Hap-Hmm € ❶ 5A

One of the best value traditional Dutch menus available in Amsterdam. A cosy and family-run institution since 1935 with simple but satisfying dishes, from €7.50. *Eerste Helmersstraat 33, T: 020 618 1884, www.hap-hmm.nl*

Chinese

Restaurant Sea Palace €€€ ❶ 2F

Amsterdam's floating Chinese restaurant, moored across from Centraal Station. High-end prices but

worth it for the experience. *Oosterdokseiland 8, T: 020 626 4777, www.seapalace.nl*

Dinner for Two

De Belhamel €€ ❶ 1C

Cosy, candlelit, contemporary cuisine in a busy restaurant and bar overlooking Brouwersgracht canal. Alfresco dining on the terrace during summer. *Brouwersgracht 60, T: 020 622 1095, www.belhamel.nl*

French & Haute Cuisine

Grand Café-Restaurant 1e klas €€€ ❷ 1E

Centraal Station's breathtaking art nouveau railway restaurant: the perfect setting for super-elegant brasserie food, an atmospheric cocktail or morning coffee. *Platform 2b, Centraal Station, T: 020 625 0131, www.restaurant1eklas.nl*

Bordewijk €€€ ❶ 1B

One of the best in Amsterdam: on a par with a Michelin-starred restaurant but significantly better value: visionary cooking. Stark modern interior and acoustics. *Closed Sun, Mon. Noordermarkt 7, T: 020 624 3899, www.bordewijk.nl*

Café Restaurant Amsterdam €€ Off map

The décor alone is worth the visit with the restaurant being located in a former water pumping station. The menu is modestly priced with the usual French suspects on offer. *Watertorenplein 6, T: 020 682 2666, www.cradam.nl*

Christophe €€€ ❶ 2B

Top chef Jean-Joël Bonsens' stylish combination of delicate French haute cuisine with subtle North African and Mediterranean accents. In a pretty canal-side location in the Jordaan: book ahead. *Closed Sun, Mon. Leliegracht 46, T: 020 625 0807, www.christophe.nl*

La Rive €€€ ❶ 6F

The Michelin star held by this restaurant in the posh Amstel hotel stands for superlative cooking using

Top-notch and elegant La Rive

the finest ingredients (truffles, game, seafood). With spectacular views across the Amstel and a soothing, gentlemen's club ambience, this place is the epitome of classic elegance. *InterContinental Amstel, Professor Tulpplein 1, T: 020 520 3264, www.restaurantlarive.com*

Fries

Vlaamse Friteshuis € ❷ 6B

Delicious, chunky Belgian fries with toppings ranging from mayonnaise

to ketchup, peanut sauce and curry. Don't be put off by the queue! *Voetboogstraat 33.*

Fusion

Beddington's €€€ ❶ 6E

Jean Beddington has long been one of the city's top chefs. English-born, trained in Japan, she has created an understated oasis in this restaurant row off the Utrechtsestraat. *Utrechtsedwarsstraat 141 (five minutes from Rembrandtplein), T: 020 620 7393, www.beddington.nl*

Recline and Dine

The Supperclub (€€ ❷ 4B) is the city's most decadent dining spot. Lie back on white-cushioned beds for unorthodox cuisine with a disco, itinerant masseurs and tarot readers. *Open daily. Jonge Roelensteeg 21, T: 020 344 6400, www.supperclub.com*

Hip & Trendy

Cobra Café €€ ❶ 7B
Named for the CoBrA (Copenhagen, Brussels, Amsterdam) art movement, this achingly popular hangout near the Museumplein serves light snacks by day and serious food at night. *Hobbemastraat 18, Museumplein, T: 020 470 0111, www.cobracafe.nl*

Utrechtsedwarstafel €€-€€€ ❶ 6E
A unique place to dine. Choose from any one of six of chef Igor Sens' seasonally-dictated 'menumatrix' options, with prices ranging from economy (three courses) to gastronome (five-course blowout). The superb wine list is overseen by Hans Verbeek. *Utrechtsedwarsstraat 107, T: 020 625 4189, www.utrechtsedwarstafel.com*

Opening Hours
Noon for lunch, as early as 5pm for dinner. Reserve tables for 7pm or 8pm. Late-night dining spots are hard to find.

Indian

Diya Indiaas Restaurant €€ Off map
Rich flavours, wonderful presentation and excellent service have made this restaurant a firm favourite. Wide range of vegetarian options also available. *Van Woustraat 240, T: 020 670 4456, www.diyarestaurant.nl*

Indonesian

Long Pura €€ ❶ 2A
Creative cuisine from various islands including Bali, Java, Sumatra and Timor, plus a sumptuous *rijsttafel*. Book well ahead. *Rozengracht 46-48, T: 020 623 8950, www.restaurant-longpura.com*

Suskasari € ❶ 3D
Like dining at an Indonesian auntie's. Authentic dishes and spicy variations. The *rijsttafels* here are fairly priced and there are vegetarian options. *Damstraat 26, T: 020 624 0092.*

Tempo Doeloe €€ ❶ 5E
Amsterdam's hottest Indonesian; bring your asbestos palate to sample some of the best and spiciest cooking in town. Reservation required. *Utrechtsestraat 75, T: 020 625 6718, www.tempodoeloerestaurant.nl*

Late-Night Munchies

De Odessa €€ Off map at ❶ 1H
If you are looking for a late-night meal and music, head to the docks east of Centraal Station and this Ukrainian fishing boat that's moored there. It has become a hip hangout where the music goes on till 3am at weekends. *Veemkade 259, T: 020 419 3010, www.de-odessa.nl*

Pata Negra €€ ❶ 6E
A shabby-chic, characterful Spanish tapas bar. It's often busy, and prices are reasonable. The kitchens here remain open later than most city restaurants (11pm midweek and 11.30pm at weekends), so it's a good option if you're after a late dinner. *Utrechtsestraat 124, T: 020 422 6250, www.pata-negra.nl*

Delicious Dutch pancakes

Pancakes

Pancakes! ① 3B
Freshly made pancakes from around the world, including traditional Dutch made from flour ground at a local windmill. Scrumptious.
Berenstraat 38, T: 020 528 9797, www.pancakesamsterdam.nl

The Pancake Bakery €€ ① 1B
Typically Dutch speciality sweet and savoury pancakes, cooked to perfection in 70 flavours and varieties.
Prinsengracht 191, T: 020 625 1333, www.pancake.nl

Surinamese

De Hapjeshoek € ① 4E
This no-frills snack bar does spicy noodle dishes and sandwiches that attract a loyal clientele. A few tables are provided if you want to sit down.
Waterlooplein 6 (inside the metro station), T: 020 423 0130.

Fish

Lucius €€€ ② 5A
Understated, deftly cooked seafood and fish served in a long, narrow dining hall with wooden seating, ceiling fans and the catch of the day featured in the main menu. *Spuistraat 247, T: 020 624 1831, www.lucius.nl*

Nevy €€€ Off map
Upmarket, with a drop-dead view over the IJ and a winning concept: choose your freshly-landed, sustainably-sourced fish and then decide on the cooking method and

A Dutch classic – pickled herring

Herring
Raw herring is a great delicacy in Amsterdam, especially when May's *nieuweharing* season comes around and the first catch of the mild *nieuwe groene haring* (new green herring) arrives at market. The Dutch have a saying: 'A herring a day keeps the doctor away.' The traditional way to eat one is to grab it by the tail, tip your head back and gulp it down in one. There are herring stands throughout the city but these three are among the best. You can also try the famous Dutch eel and tiny shrimp:

De Zeevang ② 4B
Corner of Nieuwezijds Voorburgwal 226.

Henk's Haring ② 4C
Damstraat.

Stubbe ① 1D
Haarlemmerhuis (intersection of Singel/Haarlemmerstraat).

style of cuisine. *Westerdoksdijk 40, T: 020 344 6409, www.nevy.nl*

Vis aan de Schelde €€€ Off map

Opposite the RAI Congress Centre, Amsterdam's swankiest fish restaurant offers French classics such as *bouillabaisse* alongside house specialities such as fish lasagne and Thai fish fondue on a menu that is truly pan-oceanic. *Scheldeplein 4, T: 020 675 1583, www.visaandeschelde.nl*

Steak

Restaurant Red €€ ❶ 5C

Stylish steakhouse where guests are urged to spend less time on the menu and more time enjoying their food. Simple choice of steak, lobster or both with half a dozen wines to choose from and three or four desserts. *Keizersgracht 594, T: 020 320 1824, www.restaurantred.nl*

Thai

Krua Thai Classic €€ ❷ 6D

Indonesian places are so ubiquitous that it's easy to overlook the city's

---

excellent Thai restaurants, such as this friendly, family-run place that specialises in subtly spiced fish dishes. *Staalstraat 22, T: 020 622 9533, www.kruathai.nl*

Vegetarian

De Bolhoed €€ ❶ 1B

Quirky and kitschy, with canalside tables for the summer months. Popular with locals who come for the 100 per cent organic vegetarian and vegan food with a hint of Latin flavour. Excellent selection of homemade vegan desserts. *Prinsengracht 60-62, T: 020 626 1803.*

Café Culture

Brown Cafés (*bruin kroegen*) & *Eetcafés*

The traditional Dutch tavern or 'brown café' is the embodiment of *gezelligheid*, the peculiarly Dutch mixture of charm, cosiness, coffee and conviviality all rolled up in one.

Eetcafés are brown cafés with small kitchens where short-order chefs rustle up all manner of cheap

Brown cafés are warm and inviting

and delicious breakfasts, lunches, all-day snacks and suppers.

Café de Sluyswacht ❷ 5E

Tiny, ancient lock-keeper's house (1695) opposite Rembrandthuis which leans precariously over Oude Schans canal. Renowned for its excellent tapas and always crowded. *Jodenbreestraat 1, T: 020 625 7611, www.sluyswacht.nl*

Café In t' Aepjen ❷ 2E

Dating back to the 16th century, the oldest and most atmospheric café in town, located in one of the city's last two remaining wooden houses. *Zeedijk 1.*

De Prins ❶ 2B

Hugely popular canalside *eetcafé*: come here for classic Dutch breakfasts and tasty fare. *Prinsengracht 124, T: 020 624 9382, www.deprins.nl*

Eetcafé Loetje ❶ 7B

Museum Quarter mecca for beautifully cooked steak and fries. *Johannes Vermeerstraat 52, T: 020 662 8173, www.cafeloetje.nl*

Rembrandt's local, Café de Sluyswacht

Gollem ❷ 5A

A mind-blowing 200 varieties of local and imported beer. *Raamsteeg 4, www.cafegollem.nl*

Het Molenpad ❶ 4B

This place is open until the early hours and is one of the jolliest pubs around, with a young, local crowd and simple, hearty food. *Prinsengracht 653, T: 020 625 9680, www.cafehetmolenpad.nl*

Hoppe ❷ 6A

One of the oldest and most atmospheric cafés, with a sawdust-strewn floor, barrels and bench seats. *Spui 18, T: 020 420 4420.*

't Smalle ❶ 1B

Amsterdam's prettiest brown café: a former 17th-century distillery with picturesque canalside terraces and a barge. *Egelantiersgracht 12, T: 020 623 9617, www.t-smalle.nl*

Grand Cafés

Amsterdam's sleek and ritzy grand cafés (aka 'white cafés') attract a hip and beautiful, media-savvy crowd.

Café Americain ❶ 5B

1920s hotel café with chandeliers, velvet and newspaper-strewn tables. Come for coffee or brunch with jazz on Sunday. *Amsterdam American Hotel, Leidsekade 97, T: 020 556 3000, www.cafeamericain.nl*

Café Luxembourg ❷ 6A

One of the world's great cafés, this bohemian 19th-century bar boasts waiters in starched white aprons, great cocktails and a variety of well-priced snacks. *Spuistraat 24, T: 020 620 6264, www.luxembourg.nl*

De Jaren ❷ 6C

Happening café, bar and restaurant with two vast terraces overlooking the Amstel. *Nieuwe Doelenstraat 20, T: 020 625 5771, www.cafedejaren.nl*

Grand Café l'Opera ❷ 7D

One of the city's most famous Grand

Café Americain at night

Cafés with its Art Deco interior and indoor and outdoor terraces. The ideal spot to pull up a chair and people watch. *Rembrandtplein 29, T: 020 620 4754, www.l-opera.nl*

In De Waag ❷ 4E

Amsterdam's city gate, weighhouse and 17th-century anatomical theatre houses an awesome baronial-style designer bar lit by real candelabra. *Nieuwmarkt 4, T: 020 422 7772, www.indewaag.nl*

Schiller ❶ 5D

Art Deco hotel-café with a lovely terrace and sophisticated brasserie food. *Rembrandtplein 26, T: 020 554 0723.*

Gin-tasting Houses (Proeflokalen)

Proeflokalen (tasting houses) were abundant in the 18th century, when Dutch merchants exported up to 19 million litres (4.2 million gallons) of gin (*jenever*) annually. With the demise of the Netherlands as a trading power, only a few places remain open today.

De Admiraal ❶ 3C

Laid-back with 15 kinds of gin, beer, wine; hot meals and snacks. *Herengracht 319, T: 020 625 4334, www.proeflokaaldeadmiraal.nl*

De Drie Fleschjes ❷ 3B

350 years old (look for the casks embossed with patrons' names). *Gravenstraat 18, T: 020 624 8443.*

De Ooievaar ❷ 2E

The smallest *proeflokaal* in Holland, with free plates of cheese and beef. A franchise of the city's last

> ### Doctor's Orders
>
> Made of grain and molasses and laced with juniper berries, Dutch gin (*jenever*) dates from the 17th century. *Oude* (old) gin has a smooth, aromatic, malty flavour; *jonge* (young) gin is blander but packs a strong punch. Many Amsterdammers traditionally drink their beer with a gin chaser (*kopstoot*); literally a 'smack on the head'.

Imposing entrance to In De Waag

remaining distillery, Wees, whose 10-year-old *jenever* is about as good as it gets. *Sint Olofspoort 1, T: 020 420 8004, www.de-ooievaar.nl*

Coffeeshops

The sale of soft drugs in Amsterdam's coffeeshops is tolerated as long as it remains discreet. Most serve coffee, soft drinks and snacks, while a few have alcohol licences.
No under-18s.

Barney's Off map
Amsterdam's best known coffeeshop and winner of multiple 'High Times Cup' awards. Its futuristic interior attracts visitors in their droves. Guest DJ sets on most evenings. *Haarlemmerstraat 102.*

Green House Centrum ❷ 5C
Popular haunt with its own steady stream of regulars, and the occasional A-list celebrity dropping in on occasion. *Oudezijds Voorburgwal.*

The Dope on Dope

The tolerated limit for possession of cannabis in Amsterdam is set at 5g (0.2oz) and is strictly regulated. Skunk (*nederwiet*) is cultivated indoors under lights and its THC (tetrahydrocannabinol) content is stronger than ordinary marijuana. Hash cakes are also strong; highs can take up to two hours to kick in and last up to 10 hours. Locals avoid smoking in the street (*see Smoking, p.50*) and it's polite to ask before lighting up other than in a coffeeshop.

amsterdam practical information

Built in the 17th century, Amsterdam's Grachtengordel, or 'girdle of canals', wraps around the old medieval harbourside like a cleverly constructed spider's web. Beyond the Canal Ring (Singel, Herengracht, Keizersgracht and Prinsengracht), the city fans out into Jordaan, Museum Quarter, de Pijp and Oost. Boats are the most relaxing way to get around: tourist boats stop off at all the major sights, and other maritime options include water taxis, boat-hire, water bikes (pedalos) and candlelit cruises. With its very compact centre, Amsterdam is also ideal for exploring on foot or by bicycle (though walkers should beware of the relatively silent bicycle traffic and bear in mind that in Amsterdam cleanliness is not next to godliness, and some streets offer more than their fair share of ground-level obstacle courses).

know it practical information

Tourist Info

Amsterdam Tourist Office (VVV)
2 1E, **1** 5B

There are three visitor information centres with branches located at Arrivals 2 in Schiphol Airport, *Stationsplein 10* (across from Centraal Station) and *Leidseplein 26*. The central number is *T: 020 702 6000, www.visitamsterdam.nl*

Arriving by Air

Amsterdam Airport Schiphol **4**

One of the world's most efficient and aesthetically pleasing airports, with more than 40 works of art, plus a Rijksmuseum annex on Holland Boulevard, behind Passport Control

Schiphol Airport

between E and F piers. *Open 7am-8pm daily for travelling passengers (after check-in), T: 0900 0141 (all enquiries), www.schiphol.nl*

Schiphol is 18 km (11 miles) from Amsterdam. Trains to Centraal Station leave 24 hours a day at 10-15 minute intervals; the journey takes 20 minutes and tickets cost €3.90. Another option is a taxi, which takes 20-30 minutes and costs €40-50. Connexxion shuttle coaches leave every 20 minutes and drop off at 45 hotels in the city centre (€16.50). *T: 088 339 4741, www.schipholhotelshuttle.nl*

Getting around Amsterdam

By Bike

Watch out for oncoming trams and wheel-trapping tram lines. Bike theft is very common and locks are essential at all times.

Bike City **1** 2B
Bloemgracht 70, T: 020 626 3721, www.bikecity.nl

Bicycle Thieves
Bike theft is rife in Amsterdam: in 1999, the most audacious bicycle thief ever – Chiel van Zelst – confessed to stealing more than 50,000 bikes since the 1980s, a story eagerly retold in his fascinating memoir, called *100,000 Bike Valves.*

Mac Bikes for hire

Mac Bike ❷ 1E, ❶ 5B, ❷ 7E, ❷ 6F
Branches: Centraal Station Oost, Leidseplein, Waterlooplein and Marnixstraat. T: 020 620 0985, www.macbike.nl

Canal Bikes
Slow but fun, canal bikes are one-to four-person pedalos available for hire from moorings on *Singelgracht* (Rijksmuseum, ❶ 6B), *Prinsengracht* (Westerkerk, ❶ 2B), *Keizersgracht* (Leidsestraat, ❶ 5B) and *Leidsekade* (near the American Hotel, ❶ 5B). They're particularly good fun for kids. Rental is from €8/hour, with a €20 deposit. T: 020 217 0500, www.canal.nl

By Boat

Canal Bus & Museumboot ❷ 1E
Starting from the jetty opposite Centraal Station, the Canal Bus (T: 020 217 0500, www.canal.nl) does three loops around the city: the green and red lines stop off at 19 sights between the Rijksmuseum, Leidseplein and Waterlooplein; the blue line travels west, taking in Artis

See the canals from a boat

Zoo, the Scheepvaart Museum, NEMO and the Tropenmuseum. You can hop on or hop off at any point along the route: tickets, which are valid until noon the following day, are €19.80 and include discounts on museum entrance. Following similar routes, the Museumboot and Artis Expres (T: 020 530 5412, www.lovers.nl) also commence their journey from Centraal Station: 24hr tickets cost €22 and include discounts on museums.

Taxis & Water Taxis

Taxis are expensive but easy to get hold of: look for them in taxi ranks in

Ticket to Ride
Available from the drivers, automatic dispensers, post offices and shops, the *Dagkaarten* (Day Pass) gives unlimited rides on trams, buses and metros for €7.

the main squares. Taxis cannot be flagged down, but must be entered at taxi stands, with locations around the city. The taxi queue at Centraal Station has improved recently with unlicensed 'pirate' cabs supposedly banned; these refuse short-distance rides and are known for not using their meter. Use TCA cars with sign on roof (Taxi Centrale Amsterdam): *T: 020 777 7777*. Water taxis can be expensive for small groups but reasonable for larger parties of 6-8. Contact Amsterdam Yellow Cabs for a quote: *T: 020 535 6363, www.water-taxi.nl*

Trains

Centraal Station ❷ 1E
Stationsplein 15, T: 0900 9292.

Nederlands Spoorwegen Internationale ❷ 1E
Stationsplein 15, T: 0900 9296, www.ns.nl

The beautiful brick-patterned Centraal Station

Trams, Buses & Metro

Trams are quick and convenient. Buses and metros are good for getting to the outskirts of town. The *Opstapper* bus runs round the Prinsengracht (*see Transit map*) and can be hailed anywhere along the route. If visiting for a short break, purchase an economical *OV-chipcard* from a supermarket, tourist office or ticket machine. They last for between 24 hours and 168 hours and allow unlimited travel on trams, metros and buses (including night buses) for the duration of the card. On entering your chosen mode of transport, you must remember to swipe your card (chipping in) in front of the sensor at the main door and again (chipping out) when exiting.

Metro sign

Euros

GVB ❶ 1E
Stationsplein (in Smits Koffiehuis, opposite east entrance of Centraal Station), T: 0900 8011.

Public Transport Info
Contact *9292* via *T: 0900 9292* (€0.70 per minute) or via *www.9292.nl*

Car Hire

Avis
Nassaukade 380, T: 020 683 6061.

Europcar
Overtoom 197, T: 020 683 2123.

Hertz
Overtoom 333, T: 020 612 2441.

Changing Money

Hours are Monday-Friday 9am-5pm. Banks will buy and sell travellers' cheques and currency; the commission is much higher in a bureau de change.

GWK Travelex ❷ 1E
Centraal Station and Schiphol Airport, open 8am-10pm, T: 020 627 2731.

American Express ❷ 3C
Damrak 66, T: 020 504 8770.

Disabled Access

Trams are almost inaccessible to wheelchair users (even in more modern tram cars, there's a gap of 20 cm/8 in). Only a few buses can kneel, whereas metros are fully accessible, with lifts at every station. Taxis take only folding wheelchairs; if you need to travel in your wheelchair, call Connexxion Taxi Services a day in advance, *T: 020 633 3943*. All public buildings are obliged to provide full disabled access; however, some of the older hotels don't have lifts. For information contact Amsterdam's Uitburo *T: 020 702 6100*, the Amsterdam Tourist Board (I amsterdam) *T: 020 702 6000* or ANWB Disabled Department *T: 070 314 1420*.

Emergencies

Emergency Number
Police, ambulance and fire, T: 112.

24-hour Doctor

Central Medical Service open 24 hours and will provide details on doctors in your area as well as those that can help out of hours.
T: 0900 503 2042.

24-hour Hospital

Onze Lieve Vrouwe Gasthuis ❶ 7G

Oosterpark 9, T: 020 599 9111, www.olvg.nl

24-hour Pharmacy

For the nearest 24-hour pharmacy (apotheek), T: 020 592 3315.

Internet Cafés

Bagels & Beans ❶ 5C, ❶ 7A, ❷ 7E

A stylish chain of cafés offering free internet access to customers. Branches at: Ferdinand Bolstraat 70, Keizersgracht 504, Raadhuisstraat 18, Van Baerlestraat and Waterlooplein 2, www.bagelsbeans.nl

The Mad Processor ❶ 4A

30 minutes access for €1. Kinkerstraat 13, T: 020 612 1818.

Left Luggage

There are 24-hour lockers at Centraal Station and Schiphol Airport.

Lost & Found

For insurance purposes, report lost items to the police, T: 020 559 9111.

Mail

Letters and postcards to Europe cost €0.85. Postcards outside Europe are €0.95. Stamps (postzegels) are sold in tobacconists, souvenir shops and post offices (open 9am-5pm Monday-Friday – look for blue and red 'ptt post' signs). Post going outside Amsterdam should be mailed in the slot marked 'overige bestemmingen'.

Public Phones

Most payphones take phonecards, not coins. Local calls cost €0.25 per 20 seconds. For overseas calls, use the international code (00 1 for the US or 00 44 for the UK).

To call Amsterdam from abroad, dial 011 31 20 from the US or 00 31 20 from the UK. You can dial long-distance and international calls directly from any payphone: most take phone or credit cards – phonecards are available at most major post offices and newsagents, and can be bought in units of €5, €10 and €25.

Directory Enquiries

1888 (national).
1889 (international).
€0.70 per minute.

Operator

0800 0101 (national).
0800 0410 (international).

Smoking

Smoking is banned in all public places, including restaurants, bars and cafés. The exception, at time of writing, is the coffeeshops where cannabis is sold and consumed. (Also see box, p.43.)

Tours

Bike Tours

Yellow Bike ➋ 2B
Three-hour tours or full-day trips to windmills and pancake houses (free bike rental). *Nieuwezijds Kolk 29, T: 020 620 6940, www.yellowbike.nl*

Boat Tours

Canal cruises range in price from around €9 to €50.

Blue Boat Company ➊ 6B
Stadhouderskade 30, T: 020 679 1370.

Canal Company ➊ 6C
Weteringschaus 26, T: 020 217 0500, www.canal.nl

Walking Tours

The Amsterdam Tourism & Convention Board provides a number of interesting walking tours which last between two and three-and-a-half hours. Tickets for sale at VVV information offices.

See the city on a bike tour

Summer Candlelit Cruises
Combine romance with wine, cheese or even dinner on a two- or three-hour night-time cruise round the canals with Rondvaarten (➋ 6B), *Rokin, by Allard Pierson Museum*, T: 020 625 3035.

Architecture & Art History Tours

Architectours
Custom-made architectural tours; call for details. *T: 020 625 9123.*

Artifex ➋ 6G
Expert-led tours of the Beurs van Berlage (*see p.55*), Westergasfabriek gasworks (*see p.27*) and other gems. *Rapenburgerstraat 123, T: 020 620 8112.*

Red Light District Tours

Holland Tours Schiphol
T: 020 316 3951, www.seeholland.nl

directory

This Amsterdam directory has everything you need to get the best out of the city, from annual events to finding the best hotels in all categories. There are suggestions for seeking out additional museums, galleries, parks, churches and markets, as well as some brief ideas for doable day trips from Amsterdam. You'll find titles for further reading, listings of popular websites, entertainment magazines and local newspapers, as well as a short feature on how to understand the natives.

Places to Stay

Amsterdam has more than 30,000 hotel rooms, ranging from beautiful 17th-century mansions to establishments catering for cyclists. See www.iamsterdam.com

Luxurious Hotels

InterContinental Amstel Amsterdam €€€€ ❶ 6F

This lovingly-restored riverfront palace is the jewel in Amsterdam's crown. Seventy-nine stunning rooms, many on the Amstel, plus Michelin-starred restaurant La Rive (see p.37). *Professor Tulpplein 1, T: 020 622 6060, http://amsterdam. intercontinental.com*

Key to Icons

Hotels

☜	Room Service
♟	Restaurant
♟	Fully Licensed Bar
♒	En suite Bathroom

Hotels

@	Business Centre
♨	Health Centre
❄	Air Conditioning
Ⓟ	Parking

Museums

🚻	Toilets
♿	Disabled Facilities
☕	Refreshments
🖼	Free Admission
⛩	Guided Tours

Price per room
€ budget (under €80)
€€ moderate (€80-180)
€€€ expensive (€180-350)
€€€€ deluxe (€350 +)

Hotel de l'Europe €€€€ ❷ 7C

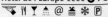

Classic 19th-century hotel overlooking the river Amstel and offering old-fashioned comforts combined with a pool and spa. *Nieuwe Doelenstraat 2-14, T: 020 531 1777, www.leurope.nl*

Okura Amsterdam €€€€ Off map

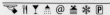

Not central, but a foodie's paradise with four restaurants including the two Michelin-starred Ciel Bleu and one Michelin-starred Yamazato (renowned as serving the best Japanese Kaiseki cuisine in the Netherlands). *Ferdinand Bolstraat 333, T: 020 678 7111, www.okura.nl*

Sofitel Amsterdam The Grand €€€€ ❷ 5C

A 16th-century convent, then a royal inn, admiralty and town hall: with a splendid inner courtyard, sumptuous rooms and a friendly staff. *Oudezijds Voorburgwal 197, T: 020 555 3111, www.thegrand.nl*

Hip Boutique Hotels

The Dylan Hotel €€€ ❶ 4B

Individually designed rooms in a beautiful 17th-century building in the heart of the nine-streets shopping district. Superb service and an intimate atmosphere. *Keizersgracht 384, T: 020 530 2010, www.dylanamsterdam.com*

Lloyd Hotel €-€€€€ Off map

The world's first 1-5 star hotel, created as an experiment by local architects and designers. The results are stunning, as modern and vintage blend seamlessly. *Oostelijke Handelskade 34, T: 020 561 3636, www.lloydhotel.com*

Maxime €€ ❶ 6B

This reasonably priced hotel has 12 stylish rooms and is just a five-minute stroll from the Museum Quarter and the Leidseplein nightlife. *P.C. Hooftstraat 63, T: 020 676 0232, www.maximeamsterdam.nl*

Classic Canalside Hotels

Ambassade Hotel €€€ ❶ 4C

One of Amsterdam's classiest and quietest hotels, spread through 10 17th-century canalside houses on the beautiful Herengracht or 'Gentlemen's Canal'. *Herengracht 341, T: 020 555 0222, www.ambassade-hotel.nl*

Hotel Pulitzer €€€€ ❶ 3B

One famous line:

Occupying a row of 17th-century canalside houses, and featuring a series of immaculately restored interiors with winding staircases, timbered ceilings and hand-painted tile walls. *Prinsengracht 315-331, T: 020 523 5235, www.pulitzeramsterdam.com*

Kamer 01 €€€ ❷ 6A

A 16th century heritage building overlooking the Singel Canal, with only two guest rooms and one suite. Owners, Peter, Wolter and Tommie the Beagle are attentive hosts, serving up gourmet five-course breakfasts. *Singel 416, T: 065 477 6151, www.kamer01.nl*

Seven One Seven €€€ ❶ 5B

Ultra-chic boutique hotel based in an 1810 mansion on Prinsengracht, beautifully decorated by super-hip designer Kees van der Valk with modern art and flea-market gems. *Prinsengracht 717, T: 020 427 0717, www.717hotel.nl*

The Toren €€€ ❶ 2B

Romantic, stylish and comfortable hotel, with a garden and only 38 rooms in two 17th-century houses situated on Keizersgracht between Dam Square and the Jordaan. They can also order food from nearby restaurant Christophe (*see p.37*) and serve it in your room or at a table. Intimate bar. *Keizersgracht 164, T: 020 622 6352, www.thetoren.nl*

Quirky Theme Hotels

Hotel de Munck € ❶ 6E

A likeable 16-room jukebox hotel based in a 17th-century sea captain's house. Decorated with Elvis kitsch and 1960s memorabilia. *Achtergracht 3, T: 020 623 6283, www.hoteldemunck.com*

Sandton Hotel De Filosoof €€ Off map ❶ at 6A

Near Vondelpark and within walking distance of the major museums, a small and simply decorated 25-room B&B dedicated to philosophy, with books on the subject in every themed room. *Anna van den Vondelstraat 6, T: 0202 681 3013, www.sandton.eu/en/amsterdam*

Boat Hotel

Blue Wave Houseboat €€ Off map

Embrace the canal life with a night or two on water, soaking up the city's atmosphere from your floating terrace (city centre a five-minute

walk). Best leave your land legs at home. *T: 020 427 8968, www.bluewavehouseboat.com*

Value Hotels

Agora €€ ❷ 7A

Attractive small hotel near the flower market, decorated with antiques: five pricier rooms overlook the Singel. *Singel 462, T: 020 627 2200, www.hotelagora.nl*

Piet Hein €€ ❶ 6A

This once unassuming hotel looking on to Vondelpark was recently transformed into a boutique hotel with budget rates. *Vossiusstraat 52-53, T: 020 662 7205, www.hotelpiethein.com*

Rho €€ ❷ 4C

Elegant and good-value hotel based in a high-ceilinged 19th-century music hall off Dam. *Nes 5-23, T: 020 620 7371, www.rhohotel.com*

Budget Hotels

Qbic € Off map

Futuristic designer pod rooms with funky lighting and free Wi-Fi. Located in the financial district with regular tram services into the city centre. *Mathijs Vermeulenpad 1, T: 043 321 1111, www.qbichotels.com*

Bed and Breakfast

Marcel's Creative Exchange €€ ❶ 5B

Stay with an Amsterdam artist who rents rooms out to artists and other city visitors, but book well ahead. No breakfast but fascinating cultural exchange guaranteed. *Leidsestraat 87, T: 020 622 9834, www.marcelamsterdam.com*

Hostels

Coco Mama € ❶ 7E

Amsterdam's first boutique hostel, housed in an old brothel. Private rooms and two- to six-bed dorms available. All mod-cons and free internet. *Westeinde 18, T: 020 627 2454, www.cocomama.nl*

Apartment Rental

If you want to stay in the city for a week or longer, renting an apartment might be a better option. Furnished apartments will set you back at least €1,000 per month, with a minimum let of usually two months, through *Apartment Services, Waalstraat 58, T: 020 672 1840, www.apartmentservices.nl*

Museums & Sights

Amsterdam's other museums. Details of main entries in *See it pp.2-13.*

Allard Pierson Museum ❷ 6B

Erudite archaeological collection with some fine Etruscan and Egyptian relics and plaster casts. *Adm. Open 10am-5pm Tue-Fri, 1pm-5pm Sat-Sun. Oude Turfmarkt 127, T: 020 525 2556, www.allardpiersonmuseum.nl*

Beurs van Berlage ❷ 2C

Amsterdam's graceful former stock exchange, designed by Hendrik Petrus Berlage, is now a cultural centre and exhibition hall. *Damrak 243, T: 020 530 4141, www.beursvanberlage.nl*

Bijbels Museum ❶ 4B

Stunning 17th-century interior of an opulent merchant's house on the Herengracht: ceiling frescoes by Jacob de Wit, the oldest kitchen in Holland, and a garden. *Adm. Open 10am-5pm Tue-Sat, 11am-5pm Sun. Herengracht 368, T: 020 624 2436, www.bijbelsmuseum.nl*

De Burcht ❷ 6H

The history of the Dutch Labour Movement (a bit specialised) in an exquisite Hendrik Berlage building. *Henri Polaklaan 9, T: 020 624 1166, www.deburcht.org*

directory

Erotic Museum ❷ 3D

The history of erotica, with drawings by Picasso and John Lennon. *Adm. Open daily 11am-1am. Oudezijds Achterburgwal 54, T: 020 623 1834, www.erotisch-museum.nl*

Kattenkabinet ❶ 5C

Quirky museum devoted entirely to cats, located in a handsome 17th-century canalside interior. *Adm. Open 10am-5pm Mon-Fri, 12noon-5pm Sat-Sun. Herengracht 497, T: 020 626 9040, www.kattenkabinet.nl*

Munttoren ❷ 7B

Part of a city gate built into the walls in the 1480s, used as a mint in the 17th century, still with its original carillon (*see p.24*). *Muntplein.*

Museum van Loon ❶ 5D

This swanky 1602 canalside house was owned by Willem van Loon, a rich trader and founder of the Dutch East India Co in the 17th century.

Adm. Open 11am-5pm Tue-Sun. Keizersgracht 672, T: 020 624 5255, www.museumvanloon.nl

Nieuwe Kerk ❷ 3B

Magnificent Gothic basilica on Dam Square, dating from 1408, with glorious stained glass: hosts exhibitions and concerts. *Dam, T: 020 638 6909, www.nieuwekerk.nl*

Oude Kerk ❷ 3D

One of Amsterdam's most fascinating churches (*see p.24*): begun in 1306 and much altered over the years but still with its original wooden roof. Its cavernous interior features a mammoth organ and stained glass. *Oudekerksplein 23, T: 020 625 8284, www.oudekerk.nl*

Poezenboot ❷ 2B

Floating home to stray and abandoned cats, kept going on donations and open only in the afternoon. *Open to public 1pm-3pm daily (closed Wed & Sun). Singel 38G,*

T: 020 625 8794, www.poezenboot.nl

Sexmuseum ❷ 2D

Everything you ever wanted to know about sex but were afraid to find out in a museum. No under-16s. *Adm. Open 9.30am-11.30pm daily. Damrak 18, T: 020 622 8376, www.sexmuseumamsterdam.nl*

Tassenmuseum Hendrikje ❶ 5D

The Museum of Bags & Purses is situated in a 17th-century canal house and presents a fascinating history of bags over the ages: their form and function, materials and decoration. Café and museum shop selling bags by young European designers.
Adm. Open 10am-5pm daily. Herengracht 573, T: 020 524 6452, www.tassenmuseum.nl

Verzetsmuseum ❶ 4G

Excellent and absorbing chronicle of the Dutch Resistance during WWII.

This museum embraces issues of persecution and local collaboration with the Germans against the Resistance and the Jews, using photographs and artefacts. *Adm. Open 10am-5pm Tue-Fri, 11am-5pm Sat-Mon. Plantage Kerklaan 61, T: 020 620 2535, www.verzetsmuseum.org*

Woonbootmuseum ① 3B

All aboard the *Hendrika Maria*, a real-life sailing barge dating from 1914: now with a small museum filled with resonant houseboat memorabilia. *Adm. Open 11am-5pm Tue-Sun Mar-Oct; 11am-5pm Fri-Sun Nov-Feb. Prinsengracht, opposite no. 296, T: 020 427 0750, www.houseboatmuseum.nl*

Parks

Vondelpark ① 6A
See p.12.

Hortus Botanicus ② 7G
In the midst of city the Hortus offers tranquillity, with lovely gardens and exotic palm trees. *Plantage Middenlaan 2a, www.hortus-botanicus.nl*

Museumplein ① 7B
Linking the Rijksmuseum (*see p.10*), Van Gogh Museum (*see p.11*), Stedelijk Museum (*see p.10*) and the Concertgebouw (*see p.24*), this top people-watching spot was revamped and landscaped by Danish architect Sven-Ingvar Andersson in 1999. As well as a wading pool, winter skating rink, grassed-over supermarket and skateboard ramp, there's the Cobra Café (*see p.38*), good for drinks and snacks by day and fêted for its transparent toilets, which frost over at the touch of a button.

Amsterdamse Bos ④
Built in the 1930s, Amsterdam's handsome *bos* (forest) is a massive 810-hectare (2,000-acre) park with an open-air theatre, bathing pools, pancake house, farm, adventure playground and horticultural museum, plus an Olympic-sized rowing lake called the Bosbaan. It's great for kids: you can hire bikes, canoes or pedalos, watch buffalo and bison roam free or take a 60-minute antique-tram ride round the perimeter. *Amstelveen (take a bus from Centraal Station), www.amsterdamsebos.nl*

Beatrixpark ④
Serene oasis with a Victorian walled garden and pond, streams and bridges: come here for outdoor concerts in July and August. *SW of the centre opposite the RAI Exhibition Centre.*

Westerpark Off map
Small and lovely, and adjacent to the Westergasfabriek gasworks (*see p.27*), an awesome landmark of Dutch industrial architecture, this is now a trendy film studios and arts complex with cafés, restaurants, exhibitions and performances. *NW of the centre, near Haarlemmerpoort.*

Markets

Find more details of the main entries in *Buy it, pp.14-21.*

Albert Cuypmarkt ① 7D
See p.20.

Amstelveld ① 6E
Plant and flower market of around 30 stalls near the Rembrandtplein.

Open 10am-3pm Mon. Prinsengracht near Utrechtsestraat.

Bloemenmarkt ❷ 7B
See p.20.

Boerenmarkt ❶ 1B
Farmers' market for fruit, vegetables, meat, bread and dairy products. *Open 9am-4pm Sat. Westerstraat-Prinsengracht.*

De Looier ❶ 4A
See p.17.

IJ Hallen Off map
See p.20.

Nieuwmarkt ❷ 4E
Organic produce, as well as antiques and books in summer months. *Open 9am-5pm Sat. Nieuwmarkt.*

Noordermarkt ❶ 1B
See p.21.

Postzegelmarkt ❷ 3B
Stamps, coins, postcards and medals. *Open 10am-4pm Wed & Sat. Nieuwezijds Voorburgwal.*

Rommelmarkt ❶ 4B
Mesmerising indoor flea-market. *Open 10am-4pm Mon-Thu & Sat-Sun. Looiersgracht 38.*

Waterlooplein ❷ 6E
See p.21.

Westermarkt ❶ 1B
Cheerful neighbourhood market in the Jordaan; household goods and clothes. Also known as Lapjesmarkt. *Open 9am-1pm Mon. Westerstraat.*

Kids' Venues

There's lots for kids to do in and around Amsterdam, but they are not always welcome in restaurants and bars, so check in advance. Find more details on main entries in *See it pp.2-13* and *Taste it, pp.34-43.*

Amsterdamse Bos ❹
See pp.32, 57.

Het Kinderkookkafe Off map
Parents get to sit back and let the kids do the cooking in this great café. *Vondelpark 6B, T: 020 625 3257, www.kinderkookkafe.nl*

Kindermuseum ❶ 5H
An annex of the Tropenmuseum: the children's museum's excellent, imaginative shows and exhibits bring to life tropical and sub-tropical cultures *(see p.11)*. Adm. *Tropenmuseum, Linnaeusstraat 2, T: 020 568 8200, www.tropenmuseum.nl*

NEMO ❶ 2G
See p.9.

Annual Events

What's on in happening Amsterdam throughout the year.

January
Chinese New Year: dragon dancing and fireworks in Nieuwmarkt.

February-March
Head of the River: rowing competition on the Amstel (fourth week).

Stille Omgang (Silent Procession): Catholics make a silent night-time procession through the Red Light District *(see p.32)* commemorating the 1385 'Miracle of Amsterdam', when a communion wafer was recovered intact from a funeral pyre. T: 020 524 6229 (end March).

April
Museum Weekend: free or reduced admission to museums all over Holland. www.museumweekend.nl

Koningsdag (King's Birthday): knees-up involving street markets, fairs and 24-hour parties (27 April, though never celebrated on a Sunday).

May

Herdenkingsdag (Remembrance Day): Two-minute silence and wreath-laying at the National Monument in Dam Square (4 May).

Bevrijdingsdag (Liberation Day): celebrating liberation from Nazi occupation: bands, speeches and a market (5 May).

Echo Grachtenloop (Canal Run): popular canal-marathon run along the length of Prinsengracht and Vijzelgracht, involving up to 5,000 people (fourth week).

June

Amsterdam Roots Festival: great programme of music and culture from around the world, with a specially built Children's Village and a children's festival, www.amsterdamroots.nl

De Grachtentuin in bloei: a number of gardens open to the public

between Brouwersgracht and the Amstel river. Rare plants and lovely gardens to be admired (late June). www.opentuinendagen.nl

Holland Festival: month-long celebration of performing art in the main music venues of Amsterdam. www.hollandfestival.nl

June-August

Vondelpark Open Air Theatre (see p.12): free drama, cabaret, dance and music performances in the afternoons and evenings throughout the summer. T: 020 673 1499.

July-August

Kwakoe Zomer Festival: Surinamese and Antillian festival with music, dance and comedy lasting for six weekends.

August

Grachtenfestival: a series of city-wide weekend celebrations with more than 70 top concerts by international musicians. Plus a special weekend for children, www.grachtenfestival.nl

Gay Pride: parades, parties, posing and outrageous performances

celebrating the city's gay community (first weekend). www.amsterdamgaypride.nl

Uitmarkt: during the last weekend of August, the stretch of the Oostelijk Havengebied (East Harbour Area) east of Centraal Station along the water hosts dance, theatre, music and literary performances to launch the new cultural season. www.uitmarkt.nl

Prinsengracht Concert at the Grachtenfestival: free canalside concert outside the Hotel Pulitzer (see p.53). T: 020 421 4542.

September

Amsterdam Fringe: 10 days of avant-garde theatre productions from all around the world. www.amsterdamfringe.nl

Amsterdam Heritage Weekend: Historical buildings, which are normally closed, are open to the public (second Saturday).

Bloemencorso: flower pageant through the city centre around Dam Square and Vijzelstraat (first week), www.aalsmeers-bloemencorso.nl

HISWA in-water Boat Show: massive boat show with yachts and motor boats of every description. *www.hiswa.nl*

Jordaan Festival: street festival. *www.jordaanfestival.nl*

November

Sint Nicolaas Parade: Santa Claus processes through the city on a white horse, accompanied by his *pieten*; helpers with blacked-out faces who are called *Zwarte Pieten* (Black Peters) (mid-November).

PAN (National Art and Antique Fair): more than 100 dealers selling top-notch old masters and covetable furniture (late November), *www.pan.nl*

December

Pakjesavond: families exchange Christmas presents to celebrate the birthday of St Nicholas (5 December).

Oudejaarsavond (New Year's Eve): raucous city-wide jamboree, with fireworks and street parties (31 December).

Public Holidays

New Year's Day (1 January).
Good Friday.
Easter Sunday & Monday.
King's Day (27 April).
Liberation Day (5 May, once every five years).
Ascension Day.
Whit Sunday & Monday.
Christmas Day (25 December).
Boxing Day (26 December).

Day Trips from Amsterdam

Other places to visit that are within easy distance of Amsterdam; all are accessible by car or public transport.

Haarlem ❹

No visit to this elegant little town, with its gabled houses and its towering church, is complete without exploring the Frans Hals Museum. Alongside the incomparable genre paintings of this great artist is a wide range of Dutch art from the 16th century to present day. *20 km (12.5 miles) west of Amsterdam. Museum: Adm. Closed Mon. Groot*

Heiligland 62, Haarlem, T: 023 511 57 75, www.franshalsmuseum.nl

Flowers/nature

Keukenhof (❹) is a dazzling shrine to the Dutch bulb-growing industry. It is is a 20-hectare (70-acre) spectacle of a flower garden that bursts into flamboyant bloom during late March to May. *35 km (22 miles) south of Amsterdam. Adm. Tours. Stationsweg 166a, Lisse, T: 0252 465555, www.keukenhof.nl*

Other destinations of interest to flower- and nature-lovers include the Museum de Zwarte Tulp in Lisse (*Open 1pm-5pm Tue-Sun. Grachtweg 2a, T: 0252 417 900, www.museumdezwartetulp.nl*), which retells the story of Dutch tulip-mania in the 1630s.

De Cruquius Museum at Cruquius (*www.cruquiusmuseum.nl*) explains the creation of the polders and dams that hold back the sea.

Nationaal Park de Hoge Veluwe
Off map

For those who want more than a day at the Van Gogh Museum (*see p.11*), the Kröller-Müller Museum has a vast collection of the artist's work, and is set in an attractive nature reserve near Apeldoorn. *Adm. Open 10am-5pm Tue-Sun. 80 km (50 miles) south-east of Amsterdam. Houtkampweg 6, Otterlo, T: 0318 59 12 41, www.kmm.nl*

Zaanse Schans ❹

Part experiment in living in 17th-century fashion and part tourist attraction, this little village comprises buildings that were relocated here from all over the Zaan region. The local inhabitants run the community as a piece of living history, operating the mustard and saw mills and the traditional craft workshops. In summer there are boat tours through the dykes. *Schansend 7, Zaandaam, T: 075 681 0000, www.zaanseschans.nl*

Listings

Amsterdam has very few listings magazines in English – pick up flyers in bars and cafés or choose from:

Time Out Amsterdam The local equivalent of cultural news magazines in other European capitals, in a monthly edition. Available at news kiosks. *www.timeout.com/amsterdam*

Uitburo An up-to-date website in Dutch, featuring events taking place throughout the city. *www.uitburo.nl*

I amsterdam The website features an easy to navigate What's On Event Guide in English. *www.iamsterdam.com*

Newspapers

English-language newspapers are available from most newsagents.

Athenaeum Nieuwscentrum ❷ 6A
Newspapers, periodicals and magazines from around the world. *Spui 14-16, T: 020 622 6248, www.athenaeum.nl*

Reading

See behind the scenes with this choice of writing, factual and fiction.

The Embarrassment of Riches, *Simon Schama*. Incisive analysis of the 17th-century Dutch psyche.

Going Dutch, *Lisa Jardine*. How Britain plundered Holland's glory.

Rembrandt's Eyes, *Simon Schama*. Enthralling biog.

Van Gogh, Letters. More illuminating than most art histories.

Anne Frank, Diary. Essential.

The Fall, *Margo Minco*. A tale by a survivor of the Holocaust.

Tulip Fever, *Deborah Moggach*. Psychodrama set in the 1630s.

The Tulip, *Anna Pavord*. The feverish history of tulip-mania.

Websites

www.amsterdam-webcams.com
Street, beach, skyline and underwater webcam views, plus live TV and radio.

www.underwateramsterdam.com
Alternative listings site in English.

www.amsterdam.info
Provides a wealth of information on the city for the discerning traveller, whatever your language.

speak it

Fortunately, most Amsterdammers speak faultless English, making it possible to get by in the city without a single 'Ik snap het niet'. Dutch is not as daunting as it first appears and any visit will be enhanced by even the vaguest grasp of this fiendish but fascinating language.

Useful phrases

hello – **dag**
see you again – **tot ziens**
bye – **dag**
yes – **ja**
no – **nee**
thank you – **dank u/bedankt**
sorry – **sorry**
excuse me – **pardon**
please – **alstublieft**
Do you speak English? – **spreekt u Engels... ?**
I don't know – **Ik weet het niet**
I don't understand – **Ik snap het niet**
My name is – **mijn naam is...**

Useful words

right – **rechts**
left – **links**
big – **groot**
small – **klein**
open – **open**
closed – **gesloten**
good – **goed**
bad – **slecht**

Days of the week

Monday – **maandag**
Tuesday – **dinsdag**
Wednesday – **woensdag**
Thursday – **donderdag**
Friday – **vrijdag**
Saturday – **zaterdarg**
Sunday – **zondag**

Numbers

1 – **een**, 2 – **twee**, 3 – **drie**,
4 – **vier**, 5 – **vijf**, 6 – **zes**,
7 – **zeven**, 8 – **acht**, 9 – **negen**,
10 – **tien**, 11 – **elf**, 12 – **twaalf**,
13 – **dertien**, 14 – **veertien**,
15 – **vijftien**, 16 – **zestien**,
17 – **zeventien**, 18 – **achttien**,
19 – **negentien**, 20 – **twintig**,
100 – **hondred**

Sightseeing

entrance – **ingang**
exit – **uitgang**
canal – **gracht**
bicycle – **fiets**
ticket – **kaartje**
toilet – **toilet**
Where? – **Waar... ?**
How much is? – **Wat kost... ?**
shop – **winkel**

Eating out

bill – **rekening**
waitress/waiter – **serveerster/ober**
breakfast – **het ontbijt**
lunch – **de lunch**
dinner – **het diner**
starter – **het voorgerecht**
main course – **het hoofdgerecht**
menu – **menukaart**
dessert – **nagerecht**

Shopping

How much is it? – **Hoeveel is het?**
Do you have...? – **Heeft u...?**
What time do you open/close?
– **Hoe laat gaat u open/dicht?**
I'm just looking, thanks – **Ik kijk alleen even, dank u**

Whilst every care has been
taken to check the accuracy of
the information in this guide,
the publishers cannot accept
responsibility for errors or
omissions or the consequences
thereof.
No part of this guide may be
reproduced without the
permission of the publishers.
Published by
Compass Maps Ltd.
www.popoutproducts.co.uk
© 2014 Compass Maps Ltd.
Written by Vanessa Letts, Mike
Gerrard. Updated by Ally
Thompson.

Pictures © Compass Maps Ltd
and John Heseltine Picture
Archive except the following
courtesy of Dreamstime: Jan
Kranendonk (A), p.10, p.19,
p.24, p.47; Radu Razvan
Gheorghe (B), p.12;
Jenifoto406 p.1; Dutchscenery
p.1; Victor Pelaez Torres p.1;

Elifranssens p.4L; Mario Savoia
p.5; Mihai-bogdan Lazar p.7L;
Shai Radoshitzky p.8;
Dinosmichail p.9; Laura Frenkel
p.13L; Isachenka p.15; Dennis
Van De Water p.16; Hasan Can
Balcioglu p.18; Bambi L.
Dingman p.20; Cbomers p.23;
Artur Bogacki p.25;
Antonfrolov p.25R;
Fredbervoets p.26; Mario
Savoia p.27; Julien Bastide
p.28-29; Allard1 p.32; Drobm
p.35; Wilfred Stanley
Sussenbach p.42L; Petar
Neychev p.48L; Richardt777
p.51. The following courtesy of
Shutterstock: Alexander
Demyanenko p.3; Dennis van
De Water p.4R; Curioso p.13R;
joymsk p.31R; Charlotte Lake
p.39L; r.martens p.39R;
bluecrayola p.45; Bokstaz
p.46L; luismonteiro p.48L;
Maryna Pleshkun p.48R. Also
Eye Film Museum p.6; and
John Lewis Marshall p.11.
Cover Images: Greg Gibb
Photography/Getty and
cjmckendry/istockphoto

This PopOut product, its
associated machinery and use
value, whether
singular or integrated within
other products, is subject to
worldwide patents granted &
pending, including EP1417665,
CN ZL02819864.6 &
CN ZL200620006638.7.
All rights reserved including
design, copyright, trademark
and associated copyright
property rights. PopOut is a
registered trademark and is
produced under license by
Compass Maps Ltd.

9716

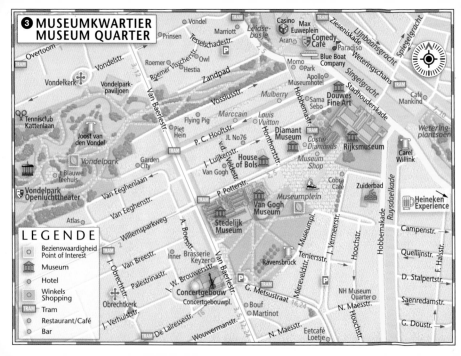

③ MUSEUMKWARTIER MUSEUM QUARTER

LEGENDE

- Bezienswaardigheid
  Point of Interest
- Museum
- Hotel
- Winkels
  Shopping
- TRAM Tram
- Restaurant/Café
- Bar

Overtoom

Vondel
Prinsen
Marriott
Tesselschadestr.
Leidse-bosje
Casino
Max Euweplein
Aran
Comedy Café
Ziesenisskade
Lijnbaansgracht
Spiegelgracht

Vondelkerk
Vondelstr.
Roemer
Roemer Visscherstr.
Owl
Hestia
Zandpad
Momo
Park
Paradiso
Blue Boat Company
Weteringschans
Singelgracht
TRAM
Café Mankind

Vondelpark-paviljoen
Van Baerlestr.
Vossiusstr.
Mulberry
Apollo
Museumhotel
Sama Sebo
Douwes Fine Art
Stadhouderskade
Weteringplantsoen

Tennisclub Kattenlaan
Joost van den Vondel
Piet Hein
Marccain
P. C. Hooftstr.
JL No76
v.d. Veldestr.
Louis Vuitton
Diamant Museum
Costa Diamonds
Rijksmuseum
Carel Willink

Flying Pig
Garden City
J. Luijkenstr.
House of Bols
Van Gogh
Thorbeckestr.
Museum Shop
Cobra Café
Zuiderbad
Heineken Experience

t Blauwe Teehuis
Van Eeghenlaan
P. Potterstr.
Van Gogh Museum
Museumplein
Ruysdaelkade

Vondelpark Openluchttheater
Atlas
Van Eeghenstr.
Willemsparkweg
Stedelijk Museum
Museumpl.
Campenstr.

A. Boesr.
J. Obrechtstr.
Inner
Brasserie Keyzer
Ravensbrück
Tenierstr.
J. Vermeerstr.
Miereveldstr.
Hoochstr.
Quellijnstr.

Van Breestr.
Palestrinastr.
J. W. Brouwersstr.
Van Baerlestr.
Concertgebouw
Concertgebouwpl.
G. Metsustraat
NH Museum Quarter
Hobbemakade
D. Stalpertstr.

Obrechtkerk
J. Verhulststr.
De Lairéssestr.
Bouf
Martinot
Wouwermanstr.
N. Maesstr.
Eetcafé Loetje
N. Maesstr.
Hoochstr.
Saenredamstr.
G. Doustr.
E. Halstr.